The Extreme Earth

Caves

Jeanne K. Hanson

Foreword by
Geoffrey H. Nash, Geologist

CHELSEA HOUSE
PUBLISHERS
An imprint of Infobase Publishing

CAVES

Chelsea House
An imprint of Infobase Publishing
132 West 31st Street
New York NY 10001

ISBN-10: 0-8160-5917-9
ISBN-13: 978-0-8160-5917-1

Library of Congress Cataloging-in-Publication Data
Hanson, Jeanne K.
    Caves / Jeanne K. Hanson; foreword by Geoffrey H. Nash.
        p. cm. — (The extreme earth)
    Includes bibliographical references and index.
    ISBN 0-8160-5917-9
    1. Caves — Juvenile literature. I. Title. II. Series.
    GB601.2.H33 2007
    551.44'7 — dc22   2006011718

Chelsea House books are available at special discounts when purchased in bulk quantities for businesses, associations, institutions, or sales promotions. Please call our Special Sales Department in New York at (212) 967-8800 or (800) 322-8755.

You can find Chelsea House on the World Wide Web at
http://www.chelseahouse.com

Text design by Erika K. Arroyo
Cover design by Dorothy M. Preston/Salvatore Luongo
Illustrations by Melissa Ericksen
Photo research by Diane K. French

Printed in the United States of America

VB FOF 10 9 8 7 6 5 4 3 2 1

This book is printed on acid-free paper.

This book is dedicated to extremophiles,
the archaic and amazing microscopic creatures
who live in extreme places like caves.

Contents

Foreword

Entering a cave is like entering a different world. Some caves bear wonderfully descriptive names such as Jewel Cave, Mystery Cave, or Talking Rocks Cave. It is easy to see why these geologic wonders sparked the imaginations of their discoverers. Caves are openings into the Earth that are environments where some ancient and unusual creatures have lived and continue to thrive.

Caves, by Jeanne K. Hanson, presents 10 examples of the main types of caves, including limestone caves, lava caves, sea caves, glacial caves, and others. Whether you want to study a limestone cave such as Mammoth Cave in Kentucky that was dissolved out of solid rock over millions of years or learn how a lava cave such as Fingal's Cave of Scotland was formed by molten rock, this book will serve as a window into a subterranean world that many people have never seen.

Of the 17,000 known caves in the United States, 150 are open to the public. Caves are scattered all over the United States and, as this book shows, all over the world. The caves described in this book might be the longest in the world, the deepest, or be distinguished by how widespread they are over a certain area. Many of the caves are the host and habitat to a class of organisms called extremophiles that, as you will see, are as old as any creatures known. These organisms can tell scientists what ancient life on Earth was like and how potential life on other planets, with their own extreme environments, might be like and how to search for it.

Caves are usually found accidentally by local people who are familiar with their natural surroundings. Sometimes caves have been found, used, forgotten, and found again across the span of thousands of years. Lascaux Cave in France is such an example. Originally found and decorated with naturalistic cave paintings of bison and deer by Ice Age Cro Magnons, the cave was forgotten until it was rediscovered in modern times. As you read about the many caves already found, imagine all the ones yet to be found, named, and studied for what they can tell us about the Earth.

As a reader, you may already have been introduced to caves through other literature. In *Tom Sawyer*, by Mark Twain, the unforgettable climax to the story took place in a cave; the comic book hero *Batman*, created by Bob Kane, uses a cave to hide his identity from the world; the smugglers in *Chitty Chitty Bang Bang*, by Ian Fleming, must have been using a sea cave for their nefarious purposes; and *Journey to the Center of the Earth*, by Jules Verne, takes readers down the most extensive imaginary cave of all.

Two recurring features of this book in The Extreme Earth set are the "In the Field" sections, which detail field methods used by geologists and other scientists such as myself to study caves, as well as the author's insights into areas of study where more research is required by future scientists. There is always something new to learn about the physical processes of our planet. The learning process, even for professional scientists, never ends, and this book will be an exciting glimpse into an otherwise dark world.

—Geoffrey H. Nash, geologist

Preface

From outer space, Earth resembles a fragile blue marble, as revealed in the famous photograph taken by the *Apollo 17* astronauts in December 1972. Eugene Cernan, Ronald Evans, and Jack Schmitt were some 28,000 miles (45,061 km) away when one of them snapped the famous picture that provided the first clear image of the planet from space.

Zoom in closer and the view is quite different. Far beneath the vast seas that give the blue marble its rich hue are soaring mountains and deep ridges. On land, more mountains and canyons come into view, rugged terrain initiated by movement beneath the Earth's crust and then sculpted by wind and water. Arid deserts and hollow caves are here too, existing in counterpoint to coursing rivers, sprawling lakes, and plummeting waterfalls.

The Extreme Earth is a set of eight books that presents the geology of these landforms, with clear explanations of their origins, histories, and structures. Similarities exist, of course, among the many mountains of the world, just as they exist among individual rivers, caves, deserts, canyons, waterfalls, lakes, ocean ridges, and trenches. Some qualify as the biggest, highest, deepest, longest, widest, oldest, or most unusual, and these are the examples singled out in this set. Each book introduces 10 superlative examples, one by one, of the individual landforms, and reveals why these landforms are never static, but always changing. Some of them are internationally known, located in populated areas. Others are in more remote locations and known primarily to people in the region. All of them are worthy of inclusion.

To some people, the ever-shifting contours of the Earth are just so much scenery. Others sit and ponder ocean ridges and undersea trenches, imagining mysteries that they can neither interact with nor examine in person. Some gaze at majestic canyons, rushing waterfalls, or placid lakes, appreciating the scenery from behind a railing, on a path, or aboard a boat. Still others climb mountains, float rivers, explore caves, and cross deserts, interacting directly with nature in a personal way.

Even people with a heightened interest in the scenic wonders of the world do not always understand the complexity of these landforms. The eight books in the Extreme Earth set provide basic information on how individual landforms came to exist and their place in the history of the planet. Here, too, is information on what makes each one unusual, what roles they play in the world today, and, in some cases, who discovered and named them. Each chapter in each volume also includes material on environmental challenges and reports on science in action, with details on field studies conducted at each site. All the books include photographs in color and black-and-white, line drawings, a glossary of scientific terms related to the text, and a listing of resources for more information.

When students who have read the eight books in the Extreme Earth set venture outdoors—whether close to home, on a family vacation, or to distant shores—they will know what they are looking at, how it got there, and what likely will happen next. They will know the stories of how lakes form, how wind and weather work together to etch mountain ranges, and how water carves canyons. These all are thrilling stories—stories that inhabitants of this planet have a responsibility to know.

The primary goal of the Extreme Earth set of books is to inform readers of all ages about the most interesting mountains, rivers, caves, deserts, canyons, waterfalls, lakes, ocean ridges, and trenches in the world. Even as these books serve to increase both understanding of the history of the planet and appreciation for all its landforms, ideally they also will encourage a sense of responsible stewardship for this magnificent blue marble.

Acknowledgments

I would like to thank Frank K. Darmstadt, executive editor, for his skillful guidance, Diane French, for her expertise as a photo researcher, and the rest of the editorial and production staff for their invaluable contributions.

Introduction

*C**aves** is written as an investigation of the planet Earth. Each of the 10 caves in the book leads backward into history, in a sense, since the top level of a cave is the oldest and the lower layers the newest. In many cases, caves are still forming on their lowest level, due to the work of water on rock, as the book will describe in each case.

The 10 caves here range widely: the world's longest cave is Mammoth Cave; the only cave related to the death of the dinosaurs is the Cenote cave system; the cave with the most amazing display of Stone Age art is Lascaux Cave; the cave with the most gigantic chamber is the Sarawak chamber of Lubang Nasib Bagus; the deepest lava cave is Kazumura; the lava cave built with the most impressive basalt columns is Fingal's Cave; the cave originally formed with the help of poison gas is Carlsbad Caverns; the cave with the most unusual "inhabitants" is Waitomo Cave; the cave with the most amazing maze is Wind Cave; and the most impressive and long-lived cave cut out of ice is Kverkfjöll. These are extreme places.

These caves range from a few thousand to a few million years old. Some are limestone, some lava, some ice, having formed out of the three most common cave materials. Limestone is, by far, the most common of all.

The caves of the book are also all over the world:

- Four are in the United States: Mammoth Cave, Kazumura Cave, Carlsbad Caverns, and Wind Cave
- One is in Central America: the Cenotes
- Three are in Europe: Lascaux Cave, Fingal's Cave, and Kverkfjöll Cave
- Two are in Asian or Pacific locations: Lubang Nasib Bagus and Waitomo Cave

Although this manuscript is a world "tour," readers of the book will also learn that most of the caves of our planet have not yet even been discovered.

Like the other books in this Extreme Earth set, this volume begins with a short chapter on the origins of caves. This chapter provides the framework, describing the main ways caves form on this planet. If you read it before beginning the book and again before launching into each chapter, you will be able to place each cave in perspective, arranging the furniture of the mind well.

Look for science-in-action. Each chapter features at least one "In the Field" section. It tells how geologists are using various techniques to study that cave today. Readers who are considering geology as a profession might even go back after finishing the book to read all of these sections again—they are always at the end of the chapter—to get a beginning sense of the field.

One thing these books will not do is settle a bet. Is the Sarawak Chamber the size of 40 Boeing 747s, or is the number found on some Web site or in some almanac the correct one? In researching this book, it quickly became evident that almost every source offered different numbers for the caves' dimensions. This is not because of carelessness or ignorance on the part of the author or the sources; rather, caves are extremely difficult to measure, and new passageways or loops are being discovered regularly. The size of chambers can be measured in various ways, by air volume and by linear dimensions, for example. The depth of a cave can be measured down to the lowest pit or the lowest passageway. The beginning and ending dates for the various broad geological periods differ among sources too. In assembling the statistics for each cave in the book, we consulted many sources and here provide the best approximations possible.

Origin of
the Landform

Caves

Most of the caves on this planet have not yet been discovered. Geologists estimate that there are literally millions more of them worldwide—and that, even in the United States, we have located only about half of our caves. About 17,000 caves are known to exist already in this country, with about 150 of these open to the public. (A listing is found in the Other Resources chapter at the end of this book.)

It is certain that Mammoth Cave in Kentucky is the prime world-record holder, and it is likely to remain so. With nearly 360 miles (580 km) of passageways discovered so far, it is the longest cave in the world. Even readers who have traveled there will be amazed to read about its geology.

Cave superlatives abound—and vary. Lists exist of the longest caves, the caves that reach down to the deepest point, the caves with the deepest single vertical drop (called a pit), the caves with the largest single chambers, the caves with the longest lava tubes created by volcanoes, and more. (No two lists are alike, and even the basic dimensions can differ from source to source.) Some caves have bats—and there is a record in that regard also; the cave with the most bats will be revealed later in this section.

These cave records change constantly, for several reasons. New caves are discovered, caves are mapped more fully or with more precise instruments, connections are found that join two known caves, and completely new areas of known caves are found for the first time. In quite a few cases, cavers have come upon vast new sections of known caves by squeezing through passages with names like Gun Barrel, Electric Armpit Crawl, and Devil's Pinch; by scuba diving down to find new openings hidden under the black water; or by improving their equipment and their nerve enough to rappel down a new pit until they hit bottom—and can get back up.

As recently as August 2004, the world record was broken again for the deepest cave pit—a straight-down drop into darkness, with surfaces impossible to climb back up without equipment. Called Velebita Cave, it is in the Velebit Mountains of Croatia, eastern Europe; this new prize-winning plunge is 1,693 feet (516 m) straight down. An impressive vertical drop, this makes that cave deeper, by far, than the Empire State Building is tall. Even with its antenna, the building is "only" 1,454 feet (443 m) tall. And not too far away from this Croatian site is another record-holder, holding firm for now: Krubera Cave (also called Voronya Cave), in the country of Georgia, once part of the Soviet Union. It winds and gradually slopes its way down to the deepest point reached by any cave, 5,130 feet (1,563 m)—almost a mile below the Earth's surface.

It is not a coincidence that these two dramatic record-breaking caves are fairly near each other. It is not a coincidence, either, that of the 35 deepest caves listed in the *Atlas of the Great Caves*, another seven are in France, nine in Spain, but none is in the United States. Neither is it a coincidence that of the 32 longest caves in this atlas, nine are indeed in our country (including Mammoth Cave). Geology is the key here, as we shall see later in this chapter and throughout the book as a whole. By the end of the book, readers will know why.

CAVE SITES

Cave science, called speleology, is studied by geologists, chemists (and geochemists), hydrologists, soil scientists, paleontologists, climatologists/meteorologists, extremophile scientists (more on that new science later in this chapter), and even public health officials. (Some 44 percent of the usable groundwater in America passes through caves, and about 25 percent of the water now pumped for drinking does so.) Cave science came into its own in the 17th and 18th centuries and has been growing ever since. There is plenty of room for future scientists to participate.

Recreationists are increasingly discovering caves too—and call them "cavers," not "spelunkers." Anyone can join a local caving club; take a cave walking tour while traveling; do "blackwater rafting," cave swims, and scuba dives; or rappel down cave pits with an organized group. Some cavers are scientists, and many more are devoted amateurs adept at mapping and discovering.

This landform has captured the imagination of people at least as far back as the days of cavemen and cavewomen, who sought shelter in these natural cavities. Native peoples on virtually every continent have used caves for safety, storage, and much else. Religious and artistic experiences have abounded in them for about 30,000 years, as have burials.

In more contemporary times, caves have served as places for small businesses, such as mushroom-growing and night-club management, and larger businesses, such as wineries. Their interiors have featured weddings, television studios, community meetings, light shows, water reservoirs, war defenses, mining, and more. Their unusual environment attracts people.

The darkness and the stable temperature—each cave's temperature hovers around the year average of its aboveground environment—have been found especially pleasant in hot climates. The first "air-conditioned" house in America got that blast of cool because it was built over a cave's mouth. It was in 1901.

Although caves are fairly common, they are also a rare resource in a sense. The overall volume of all the limestone caves on the planet (the most common type, as the book shall describe) is only about 12 cubic miles (50 km³). It takes thousands of years to create even a tiny cave, millions of years to make a big one. (Mammoth Cave required about 2 million years to form.)

Caves do not last forever either. Their roofs often cave in over time, and most of the caves on our planet have been in place for fewer than 10 million years. (This is a far shorter life span than, for example, mountains.) Cave creature species can become extinct easily, too, since the species who live only in caves—and there are thousands of them—do not have a huge population when compared with the average aboveground species. Large-scale churning of the Earth's *crust*, at least, is only a minor factor in cave destruction. The planet's crust is approximately 30 miles (50 km) thick on land and does not change much on timescales of less than millions or even billions of years.

TYPES OF CAVES: LIMESTONE DISSOLUTION

Seven main types of caves exist, as distinguished by the geology of their formation. The first two types to be described below—both variants of the limestone cave—form by the dissolution (dissolving) of this rock. One involves carbonic acid, the other sulfuric acid. These are by far the most common types of cave and usually feature the *speleothems* one thinks of first in connection with caves (*stalactites* and *stalagmites*, for example).

The first and most common type of the limestone dissolution cave forms as a slightly acidic water called carbonic acid erodes the limestone. Mammoth Cave is a superb example. Caves that form in this way can be very deep and contain substantial chambers or rooms. A large limestone cave requires about 1 million years to form, since dissolving solid rock with water is far from instant. Contrary to what many people think, these caves are not formed by a river eating its way through solid rock—the river usually enters the picture later. Instead, water from the surface slowly seeps down, through many tiny but growing cracks in the rock, until it reaches the *water table*. Limestone rock, unlike many other types of rock, will indeed dissolve in the presence of this seeping, carbonic acid water.

This "cave-making" water derives its acid from natural soils decaying gradually on the surface. And the limestone that receives it came originally from the fossilized bodies of sea animals and sea plants. These marine creatures made their shells and other hard body parts by drawing calcium carbonate out of the ocean water. So the carbonate is present in the limestone rock, ready to be dissolved back out again under the right conditions.

"Limestone caves" are also found in marble, since marble is limestone that had plunged deeper in the Earth and was subjected there to the especially high heat and pressure. This process happens through *plate tectonics*.

The reason that limestone dissolution caves are so common is because dead-sea creatures are common. Life of this kind began in the sea with a few species a couple of billion years ago and had proliferated vastly by 650 million years ago, well before it existed on land. The skeletal remains of these marine creatures began to accumulate to great thicknesses, without sediments from the continents mixed in to any great degree. The resulting compacted material is called limestone. Over the ages, through plate tectonics, masses of these fossilized sea creatures have been shoved and uplifted onto the land. The oceans have also risen and fallen over the eons, exposing yet more of the limestone.

Limestone rock masses are concentrated in areas called *karst* landscapes. The area around Mammoth Cave is one that extends over several states, as does Croatia, where the world-record deep caves mentioned earlier in this section are found.

Several of the chapters in this book feature limestone dissolution caves of this carbonic acid type:

- Chapter 1: Mammoth Cave of Kentucky, the United States;
- Chapter 2: Cenotes, Chicxulub, and the Caves of Yucatán, Mexico;
- Chapter 3: Lascaux Cave of France;
- Chapter 4: Lubang Nasib Bagus and the Sarawak Chamber of Malaysia;
- Chapter 8: Waitomo Cave of New Zealand; and
- Chapter 9: Wind Cave of South Dakota, the United States, all describe limestone caves of the carbonic acid type.

The second main type of limestone dissolution cave varies in one way: The acid that acts on the stone is not carbonic acid but rather sulfuric acid. This acid derives from layers of oil and natural gas or oil sands found underground mixed with groundwater. This process tends to form passages and chambers slightly different from those in the first type of limestone cave. This geology created Carlsbad Caverns of New Mexico and will be featured in chapter 7.

Erosion can also form caves in chalk, volcanic granite and gneiss, and gypsum. Since the geological formation process in these situations does not differ from that in limestone, caves like these will be covered only with occasional mentions.

TYPES OF CAVES: LAVA CAVES, SEA CAVES, SANDSTONE CAVES

The third type of cave, the lava cave, is completely different. Lava tube caves are formed out of moving rivers of lava flowing like tongues across the Earth's surface after a nearby volcanic eruption. The exposed surfaces of the lava harden more quickly than the lower layers. These firmer surfaces begin to hold their shape, like a subway station roof and walls, as the magma slides along inside, like the train. The inner layers of lava eventually flow out, leaving an empty tube. When part of the roof collapses, an opening for the cave is created.

Lava caves are not rare and can often be much longer than one might imagine. Some are quite dramatic, though their roofs tend to collapse into a line of rubble within only a few thousand years. Chapter 5 features Kazumura Cave of Hawaii, which is more than 40 miles (60 km) long. (The author has crawled through a few small lava tubes and hiked and scrambled through one large one, all in Iceland, another predominantly volcanic landscape.)

The next type of cave is the sea cave, which may be open either above or below the water's surface. These form above the water level at the base of cliffs when ocean or lake water erodes out an area of softer rock, leaving the harder rock around it. As the topography of the area changes through plate tectonics, some caves become entirely submerged below water level. Scuba divers have found many of them below the surface. Others rise above water level. Chapter 6 will feature Fingal's Cave on the island of Staffa, off the Scottish coast, as an example of this type. Its main composition is of ancient lava, basalt rock.

The fifth type of cave, the sandstone cave, is quite common. Like sea caves, these form at the base of cliffs where water dissolves the rock, in this case sandstone. This common rock can be so soft that a person's hand can "erode" it, scratch it away. Sandstone caves tend to be shallow and dry, making them appealing to humans for eons. The Mesa Verde Cliff Dwellings in Colorado were built as sandstone caves. Since sandstone caves tend to be quite shallow and not geologically complex, the book does not devote a chapter to them.

TYPES OF CAVES: GLACIAL CAVES, TECTONIC CAVES

The sixth type of cave, the glacial cave, is constructed out of solid ice within the body of a glacier. The cave is cut by flowing water, usually in summertime. By winter, new construction usually ceases and refreezing water fills part or all of the cave. Since glaciers move, these caves are also unstable even when open and reasonably accessible. House-size boulders can be propelled off a wall by a shift—otherwise entirely silent—in the ice wall as the glacier flexes. Glacial caves tend to last a few days, years, or decades. New ones are always forming, however. Some glacial caves form and reform in about the same place each summer, while others do not. Chapter 10, on Kverkfjöll Cave of the Vatnajökull Glacier, Iceland, will serve as an example of this type of cave.

The seventh type of cave, tectonically formed, is created by a sudden large-scale movement of rock masses, the kind of movement created by an earthquake, for example. This type of cave, uncommon, is not featured as a separate chapter.

Of course, there are also artificial caves, hollowed out by people for specific uses. Kansas City has parking garages inside old salt caves, and the Soviet Union conducted top secret weapons research in a Siberian cave. Natural salt caves, though rather rare since salt is so soluble in water, are found in Israel and in other locations. And of course caves have been excavated for the storage of wine.

CAVES FEATURED

The caves chosen for inclusion in this book were selected because of their typical, yet amazing, geology. Consideration was given to choosing ones in the United States, which can be visited, balanced with others in a variety of more far-flung locations. Not every cave included is a record-holder for size, though one holds the most complex maze, another the deepest lava tube cave, and one is home to the largest chamber—large enough to hold several airplanes. Readers will need to read the book to find out which is which.

Readers will also learn in this book about the amazing new science devoted to extremophiles. These tiny organisms, if added together, would probably weigh more than all of the surface organisms found on our planet. Many of the chapters will devote some space to these unusual creatures that thrive in inhospitable conditions and may well have been the earliest life-forms on Earth. Extremophiles can still be found in unusual environments such as caves, and new discoveries are made by scientists regularly. This is a frontier in science in which readers may choose to participate.

One other factor was considered: The cave with the most bats was *not* included. But about 20 million of these useful, insect-eating creatures—the largest colony discovered so far—live in Bracken Cave, central Texas.

Mammoth Cave of Kentucky

United States

Mammoth Cave conceals the River Styx, Fat Man's Misery, the Rotunda, Little Bat Room, Bottomless Pit, Relief Hall, Cathedral Dome, Echo River, and Frozen Niagara, along with dozens and dozens of other named features. Visitors can descend to walk through all of them, as this is a national park.

There is plenty of room here: Mammoth Cave's passageways add up to nearly 360 underground miles (580 km). Only about 160 miles (258 km) of these have been thoroughly mapped. And geologists estimate that perhaps hundreds of miles remain to be discovered, even here in the United States' most famous cave. Hidden passages and chambers can easily lie behind various blockages of rock at the ends of exceedingly narrow known passageways. The cave loops through five or six different levels, depending upon how the elevations are distinguished. Its formation was—and is—amazing and complex.

Even without any more discoveries, Mammoth Cave is the longest cave in the world—about three times longer than its nearest competitor. As will be seen in this chapter, a cave this long is always cut from limestone. (Please see the introductory chapter Origins of the Landform: Caves, to place limestone caves in perspective.)

Mammoth Cave was not built in a year, or even in a few million years. In fact, it required about 30 million years to carve the 350-million-year-old limestone that existed here into this geological sculpture decorated with formations. Because construction required erosion, the oldest rocks remaining here are "only" about 2 million years old. Erosion by dissolution at Mammoth, and in many caves, reaches the level of art.

SOME CAVE RECORDS

Mammoth Cave, though the longest cave in the world, has some quite impressive runners-up. From *Atlas of the Great Caves of the World*—its most recent numbers based upon measurements completed in 1989—here are the top 10:

10.	Zoluška, Ukraine	269,028 feet	(82,000 m)
9.	Wind Cave, South Dakota, the United States	269,271 feet	(82,074 m)
8.	sistema de Ojo Guareña, Spain	292,227 feet	(89,071 m)
7.	système de la Coumo d'Hyouernèdo, France	296,903 feet	(90,496 m)
6.	Ozernaja, Ukraine	351,050 feet	(107,000 m)
5.	Siebenhengste-Hohgant-Hölensystem, Swizterland	360,892 feet	(110,000 m)
4.	Jewel Cave, South Dakota, the United States	406,073 feet	(123,771 m)
3.	Hölloch, Switzerland	433,516 feet	(133,050 m)
2.	Optimističeskaja, Ukraine	541,339 feet	(165,000 m)
1.	Mammoth Cave System, Kentucky, the United States	1,738,845 feet	(530,000 m)

In comparison with the rocks making up other limestone caves, Mammoth is also the cave with the seventh-oldest limestone. (That is not the same as the dates when a cave itself began to form out of the old rock.)

CAVE	GEOLOGIC PERIOD	APPROXIMATE AGE (MILLIONS OF YEARS)
Florida Caverns, Florida	Tertiary	50
Caverns of Sonora, Texas	Cretaceous	100
Aven Armand, France	Jurassic	150
Oregon Caves, Oregon	Triassic	200
Carlsbad Cavern, New Mexico	Permian	250
Spanish Cave, Colorado	Pennsylvanian	300
Mammoth Cave, Kentucky	Mississippian	375
Howe Caverns, New York	Devonian	375
Perry Cave, Ohio	Silurian	425
Luray Caverns, Virginia	Ordovician	450
Lehman Caves, Nevada	Cambrian	550
Eldons Cave, Massachusetts	Precambrian	1000

EXPLORATION

About 4,000 years ago, Mammoth Cave was first discovered, explored, and used by prehistoric Indians. They mined gypsum rock, took shelter, and sometimes buried their dead inside. As their culture faded, so did human knowledge of Mammoth. It was not until the 1790s that a hunter pursuing a bear discovered it again. (The bears surely knew about it all along.) Since then, two more natural entrances have been found and another 18 openings constructed for convenience.

During modern times, this cave has seen the mining of saltpeter, used to make gunpowder, especially during the War of 1812. Throughout the first third of the 1800s, it gradually became a tourist attraction. More and more miles of passageways were also discovered. One of the early guides was a slave who had taught himself to read and write, learned some geology, and led groups not only on tours but also to discover new passageways—this beginning when he was just 17 years old.

In 1926, Mammoth Cave, along with its aboveground environs, became a national park. About halfway between Louisville and Nashville in Kentucky, it is visited by about 2 million people a year and is open every day but Christmas. A visitor, dwarfed by some of its dramatic cave formations, can be seen in the color insert on page C-1. Its 10 miles of underground public trails are covered by about a dozen different tours. Most traverse broad "sidewalks," lit by electric lights. Some visitors enjoy the tour that includes the underground cafeteria lunch, in a chamber nearly as large as a high school gym.

Cave temperatures, here and elsewhere, hover around the temperature aboveground in their location, averaged across the whole year. Here inside Mammoth, that is about 54°F (12°C), year around.

BASICS OF FORMATION

A limestone cave such as Mammoth begins with a huge mass of underground limestone. This rock is the fossilized and consolidated bodies of sea creatures—everything from microscopic shells, to the bones and scales of fish, to whole coral reefs. Some of the shells, not completely crushed by pressure from above them, can be seen—and dated by geologists—in the underground rock.

The sea creatures lived here when south-central Kentucky was under a warm, ancient ocean and lying about 10° south of the equator—at a time during the *Paleozoic* Epoch called the Mississippian period. The warmer the water, generally, the broader the coral reefs and the thicker the shells of the marine organisms. Much of the coral found as rock here is more than 300 million years old and some, the horn coral, is about 570 million years old. As will be mentioned in this chapter and others, *plate tectonics* has been remodeling the landmasses and oceans of this planet for nearly 3 billion years. Nothing is now where it once was.

As the sea creatures died, their remains sank and formed an ooze, which settled and solidified over time, under the weight of the layers above. The predominant chemical composing them is calcium carbonate. The living creatures had drawn it out of the ocean water to form their shells and other body parts to begin. Gradually, the limestone was built.

Limestone is a "soft" rock, quite porous and very erodable. Though it does not look like it, limestone is actually almost as porous as gravel and sand. The mineral calcite within it erodes out the most readily.

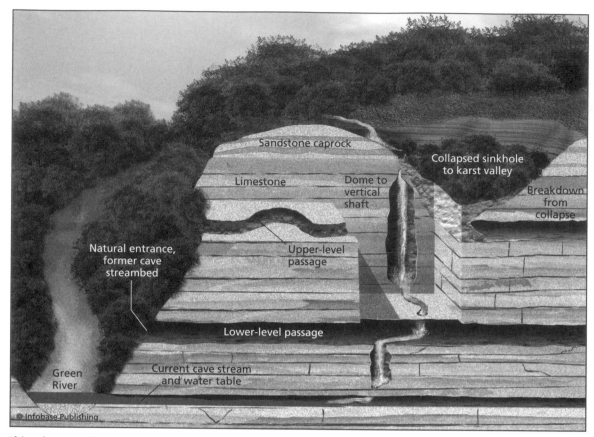

This schematic shows the basic layers of rock in Mammoth Cave, including two of the layers of passageways.

Limestone is hardly rare around the world. After all, warm seas and millions of sea creatures living in them have never been rare (and are not rare now). In fact, sea creatures such as these have been the most common, easily observable life-forms on the planet for nearly 3 billion years. They lived, generation after generation and species after species, for hundreds of millions of years before there was significant solid land or anything on it. Out in the mid-ocean today, the process of limestone formation still continues. But, though limestone is common, caves are not. Cave formation requires additional factors.

EROSION SITUATION

The limestone lay here for millions of years before the next step of evolution: rivers. Rivers, flowing across the surface of what is now Kentucky, deposited a thick layer of sand, mud, and gravel over the limestone after the seas receded. These continental *sediments* consolidated into sandstone, shale, and a mixed rock called conglomerate. This rock is actually considerably harder than limestone. It formed a lid over the limestone.

Ages passed, the dinosaurs roamed the land, then disappeared, as did the early mammals after them. (Evidence of them still existed until about 5 million years ago, when those rocks were eroded.) But yet another step was required before cave construction could begin: the cracking of the rock.

Plate tectonic processes stressed the rock over the extensive Mississippi Basin. South-central Kentucky was tilted down and toward the northwest. This "flexing" of the rock cracked it in many places. The cracks, all small to begin with, were both horizontal and vertical.

The climate changed and the rivers shifted, exposing the dry land. Finally, cave building was about to begin.

Rainwater, along with melted snow, became the sculptor. The water began to drip down from the surface, finding the cracks in the rock, both the vertical fissures and the horizontal ones at the *bedding planes* where one rock mass meets another. The water table was lowering during this period (and it always lowers in a given area as surface streams cut more deeply into the ground); this encouraged the drips to move gradually lower and lower through more rock, finding and gradually enlarging the cracks as the water percolated.

Caves form at the water table level and just below it, in what is called the *zone of saturation*. Water and rock are in maximum interaction in this zone. When one level of cave forms, there is room for the water table to drop, and then cave "construction" can begin next at that level. So the oldest levels of a limestone cave are always the ones on top. They have been left high and dry, the water having completed its job.

ACID NEEDED

Pure water by itself does not dissolve limestone. Rainwater, though, includes carbon dioxide from the atmosphere and, even more importantly, from the soil. The carbon dioxide tends to build up as surface plants decay. This mixture makes carbonic acid. It is only slightly acidic, only about one-hundredth as strong as an ordinary soft drink (the carbon dioxide is what makes the fizz). But that small amount is enough. (Limestone's potential to be eroded can be seen by placing a chip of limestone or marble in a small dish with dilute hydrochloric acid. The rock will start to bubble away.)

As the mildly acidic rainwater gradually drips down through the cracks, the rock it touches dissolves slowly. Over time, some of these cracks become wider and wider, again, both the vertical and the horizontal ones. This lets in yet more water and allows it to gather force, increasing the turbulence and corrosion, which then leads to yet more erosion.

Typically, when a crack becomes about .2 inch (5 cm) in diameter, erosion speeds up as more water flows through.

Eventually, underground streams and even rivers can flow into a cave. Waterfalls form in places, as one level of water seeks a lower level. This vertical flow eventually forms the deep *pits* within the cave.

One such pit in Mammoth is 192 feet (58.5 m) deep. The horizontal flows carved out the passageways that now can be strolled. After eons of this, many of the vertical passages intersected with the horizontal ones, creating the maze that is this "amazing" cave today.

TIME

Time is the sculptor of a cave, along with the water. The formation of Mammoth Cave took about 30 million years of dripping. During all of this time, most of the harder stone lid held up the roof without collapse. If it had not, the cave would have become only a pile of boulders (a huge pile). Of course, there is always some collapsing, usually of only part of the roof (creating boulder fields inside) but sometimes of a large section of roof (providing new openings to the cave system). The reason that caves do not last forever is because eventually all rock will collapse. Limestone caves, however, often last millions of years.

During this time north of the Mammoth Cave area, the glaciers expanded and contracted aboveground. Though they never reached this far south, their meltwater did. During the warmer periods of the *Pleistocene*, floodwaters entered Mammoth Cave, helping to enlarge both the vertical and horizontal spaces. Even now, in times of flood, the waters of the Green River enter the cave.

SHAPE OF THE CAVE

Geologists can tell, simply by examining the layout of Mammoth Cave, that it formed more by dripping water than by raging rivers. A cave made by a river or stream would be laid out like the trunk, branches, and twigs of a tree, as is an aboveground river and stream tributary system. A cave made more by dripping water is patterned, as here, more like a city's street map. One crack intersects another at roughly right angles, as streets often do. Of course, both kinds of water flow are generally present to some degree.

Both the dripping and the flowing water are also the creators, in a different way, of the *speleothems—stalactites* and *stalagmites*, for example. This process and the formations that result will be described later in this chapter and covered further in all the chapters that feature limestone caves, since it involves such variety. An example of the size these formations can take can be seen in the color insert on page C-1.

In studying a cave, geologists and cavers also look for layers of rock that are not limestone. That rock, harder to erode, sometimes forms the roof or floor of an interior limestone passageway (as it does the roof of the whole cave). This layer can conceal hidden passages, and following it can lead to them.

Cave explorers also pay attention to how and where a cave "breathes." If air movement is detected, that means areas of the cave are equalizing their air pressure. This effect often indicates undiscovered areas of the cave. The breathing cave phenomenon will be described further in chapter 9, which covers the Wind Cave of South Dakota.

LIMESTONE/KARST

Limestone—and its related rocks marble, gypsum, dolostone, and even chalk—are not rare, as has been discussed. These rocks are, in fact, the world's largest store of carbon. (The location of these rock masses also leads geologists to insights about the location of the ancient seas that left a lot of limestone as the sea creatures died, and even about ancient climate.) These now-underground limestone areas are also usually seen at the surface too. Called *karst terrain* when seen at the surface, the name comes from the Kars area of Croatia.

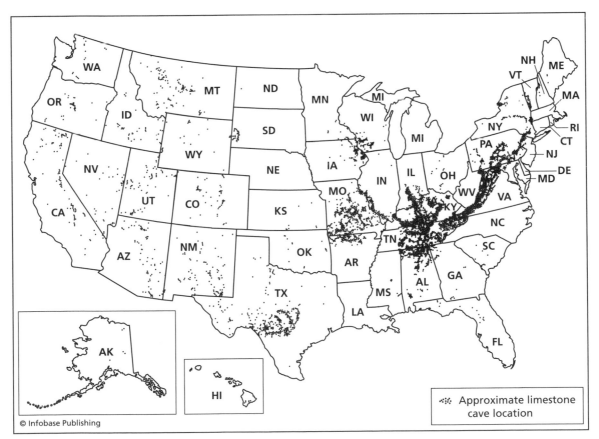

© Infobase Publishing

This map shows that limestone caves in karst terrains are not rare in the United States, particularly in certain areas.

Karst covers large swaths of Kentucky, Tennessee, Indiana, Missouri, and Arkansas, Mammoth Cave's broad "neighborhood" area within the United States. Also, western New York State, West Virginia, Georgia, and Florida have extensive areas of karst terrain. The state of Georgia is home to the deepest cave in this country, a cave which also has the deepest pit in the United States, Ellison's Cave. The state of Florida is about one-third karst and even has caves underwater (as ocean levels rise, they "drown" caves that had formed earlier, on dry land). There are so many deep-pit caves in Tennessee-Alabama-Georgia that cavers have a nickname for this favorite region: TAG.

Around the world, karst is often but not always near the ocean's present edge. Polar regions, even on the ocean, are low in limestone, and, when it is indeed found there, caves scarcely ever form. This is because there is not enough water dripping—it is frozen instead—and soil layers and surface plants are also minimal, supplying little carbon. Hot desert regions are also infrequent locations for limestone caves, even when near the sea. There is just not enough water to drip down to dissolve rock. (Carlsbad Caverns, which may seem like an exception, provides a twist that will be discussed in chapter 7.)

Some of the best places for cave formation are within the karst terrains of the tropics. Here, plenty of water exists to drip down all year long to create erosion. And glaciers were never present to put the entire system into cold storage. Caves like this are the subjects of chapter 2, on Cenotes, Chicxulub, and the Caves of Yucatán, Mexico, and of chapter 4, on Lubang Nasib Bagus and the Sarawak Chamber of Malaysia.

KARST ON THE SURFACE

It is usually possible to recognize karst terrains, the likely home of limestone caves, by their surface features. *Sinkholes* are probably the easiest to spot, large or small, since they come in groups. Central Kentucky has about 60,000 sinkholes and southern Indiana about 300,000 of these circular depressions in the ground. The ones in the Mammoth Cave area are usually three to six feet (1 to 2 m) deep or up to 165 feet (50 m) deep.

In places such as Florida—where water is regularly pumped up from *aquifers* for drinking and where the water table has then dropped—huge, gaping sinkholes often collapse down from the surface. They can "eat" whole houses. Sinkholes usually range from up to 300 feet (91 m) to 3,000 feet (914 m) wide and up to 100 feet (30.5 m) to 900 feet (274 m) deep. There are millions around the world. Most have dimensions such that the diameter is about three times the depth. In an area, expanding sinkholes that then merge with each other are a significant force in weakening a cave's roof and causing, eventually, its complete collapse.

Other signs of a karst terrain are streams that suddenly disappear right into the ground or appear suddenly out of the ground. Mountains shaped like needles or towers, and hills shaped like cones are also signs of karst, since erosion of the soft limestone rock can make these features. And, of course, cave openings are a signal of a karst terrain. At Mammoth, the flowing water lies under the Pennyroyal Plateau, flows through underground rivers, and then emerges again at the surface at the River Styx and Echo Rivers spring, joining the Green River aboveground.

Karst terrains are of tremendous geological significance, and they have had important effects on human culture too. Rainfall that quickly drips deep into the ground in thousands of places means that less water is held conveniently near the surface for agriculture and drinking. Thinner and more impoverished soil layers can also become a problem in karst terrain since soils are drained of their nutrients by the down-dripping water. In areas of lower precipitation, karst areas can even eventually become "badlands" with amazing and intricate surface formations but scant potential for human habitation. More on karst terrains will be presented in the other chapters featuring limestone caves.

CAVE CONDITIONS FOR SPELEOTHEMS

Conditions inside the cave must be right before speleothems can form. The stalactites, stalagmites, and all the other ornate shapes of a cave cannot form when a cave is young.

The first condition must be time, since these formations are built drop by drop, trickle and ooze by trickle and ooze. In Mammoth Cave, the oldest level—remember that that is the highest one—finished forming at least 3 million years ago. The youngest level—the lowest one—is at least 100,000 years of age. Higher levels, and older caves in general, tend to have the most elaborate formations.

The second condition, which accompanies the first, is dryness. Cave areas must be exposed to air for the chemistry of speleothems to begin. They never form underwater, though they can be drowned underwater later, when conditions change.

Next is the continued entrance of water—dripping or flowing—at a slow pace. Rushing water would simply wash away these delicate "sculptures" before they could develop enough to be visible. Mammoth Cave does have rushing water after major rainstorms when the Green River enters the cave, and there the water may build more cave but also interfere with the speleothems.

Temperature, humidity, impurities in the rock, and the number of cracks in the rock also affect the ornateness of the structures. A warmer, more humid cave with lots of cracks through which water can drip means more speleothems. For those who have visited Mammoth Cave, it may sound unbelievable, but this cave is not considered especially rich in them. Its lid is a little thicker than that of other limestone caves, making it a bit harder for the drips to enter.

HOW SPELEOTHEMS FORM

Once the conditions are set, the formation of these cave decorations happens in the reverse way from how the cave itself forms. Caves form by the dissolution, the dissolving, of rock by groundwater. Think of it as a subtraction of material. The speleothems in the caves form by precipitation of calcium carbonate out of the water as it drips over rock, leaving the solid residue of the water as it evaporates. Think of it as an addition.

Here is how it works: Upper levels of the cave become dryer as cave construction moves to lower levels. The carbon dioxide in the groundwater slowly dissolves the limestone as cave construction continues. As the water moves over the cave's limestone walls and drips off, some of the water evaporates, leaving behind the calcium carbonate. This calcium carbonate builds up to form the speleothems. (The carbon is released only when the carbon dioxide in the water encounters air, much as a soda can bubbles out its carbon dioxide only when the can is opened.)

The two basic types of speleothems are *dripstone* (made by slow dripping) and *flowstone* (made by slow flowing). Examples of dripstone include stalactites and stalagmites, and an example of flowstone is a scalloped, drapery-like structure often called a scallop field.

SPELEOTHEMS: STALACTITES, STALAGMITES

These most famous speleothems are far from the only ones. In various chapters of the book, still others will be described: cave pearls, moon rocks, draperies, helictites, cave popcorn, boxwork, bacon, and organ pipes are only a few examples. (Sections of chapters in the book describing them will be labeled as variant of "Speleothems.") No two formations are ever alike, as can be seen in the color insert on page C-1.

Stalactites (think of "c" as in *icicles*) hang down from cave ceilings, like icicles. They grow as drips of water emerge from a small ceiling crack, each drip with an invisible ring of the calcite precipitated out upon contact with the air. Each of these tiny rings forms a layer of what slowly becomes a hollow tube often called a "soda straw" of calcite, as the water—slightly warmed, under a bit less pressure, and slightly agitated—has been pushed enough to begin the precipitation of its minerals out. It falls toward the cave floor, though it does not reach it in this scenario, also evaporating slightly in the process. This leaves a tiny calcite crystal, the beginning of a stalactite. The hollow tubes are delicate: Their walls are usually only about .02 inch (.5 cm) thick. Later they can become plugged and appear solid, and they can thicken as water flows along their exterior depositing crystals, but the original thin channel still remains inside.

The water hitting the cave floor under the stalactites is what builds the stalagmites. (Think of "g" as in *ground*.) This water, moving a bit too

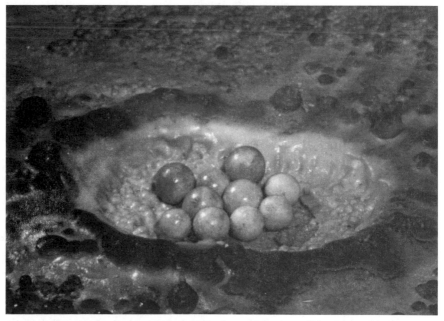

Cave pearls are an amazing kind of speleothem. *(Courtesy of the National Park Service)*

fast to evaporate completely, also still contains some carbonate rock. As it splashes down, it finally does evaporate, leaving not the tube shape of its "ceiling cousin" but more like a small splat. This drives off the remaining carbon dioxide, leaving the precipitate. Hence, stalagtites are tubular. The flatter-topped ones form in bigger splats, which can mean that the ceiling was or is farther away.

When a stalactite and a stalagmite join, a column is formed. That column thickens as the whole process continues. At Mammoth Cave, the growth rate of both formations is about .4 inch (1 cm) per year. Given enough eons, these columns can grow to be 50 feet (15.25 m) or more high and more than 25 feet (7.6 m) across. The highest parts of a cave, nearer the carbon dioxide–rich dripping water and there for a long period of time, tend to have the largest speleothems. But too much carbon dioxide in the water, unless precipitated out, can also begin to dissolve the formations.

So the process is quite delicate. It should go without saying that disturbing or destroying a speleothem would be heedless of nature and unpleasantly self-centered. And cave explorers try to avoid touching them at all.

LARGER-SCALE CAVE FEATURES

Taken at large scale, the shapes of the passageways and shafts of a cave show how the water created it. Narrow canyons are made by faster-moving streams that eventually flowed through as all the dripping areas pooled their water. Water flows faster in narrow spaces above the water table. Tubelike passageways form because they were completely filled by water, at or near the water table level. Shafts, also called pits and dome pits, are created as water moves straight down, often under a sinkhole or interior waterfall.

The largest-scale cave features of all were made before the above-ground surface became pitted with sinkholes, since surface rivers were larger then and could enter the cave as a single flow. These are generally at the higher or older levels. Since a cave's ceiling is always collapsing a bit, boulder fields can sometimes interfere with seeing all this clearly. But Mammoth Cave indeed has all these large features.

It also could easily have the most surprising and tiniest "feature" of all: living *extremophiles* and fossilized extremophiles. These creatures, now at the center of a whole new focus of geology, will be described in this chapter and in several others throughout the book.

EXTREMOPHILES: AMAZING CREATURES

This is a creature that almost no one has heard of. Even scientific articles occasionally call them bacteria or microbes, though they are not the same as bacteria, and not all of them are microbes. On our planet, they can live as deep down as 6.2 miles (10 km) under the oceanic *crust*. If placed in a pile and weighed, they would probably outweigh the total life on the surface of the Earth (from all the grass, trees, and insects up through elephants and humans). There are a lot of these tiny extremophiles, and they probably will be discovered in most or all caves, though they have not yet been searched for everywhere.

Extremophiles are ancient species. Fossilized ones have been dated at up to about 250 million years old. They will probably be found eventually to be as old as 4 billion years, geologists think. This would place them in the early eras when the Earth was without oxygen. The Earth was fiery hot then, bombarded by meteors, ultraviolet radiation, and cosmic rays and besieged with massive volcanic eruptions and torrential rains that did not relent for millions of years at a time. Different areas were very hot, or very salty, or very alkaline, or very acidic. Only extreme life-forms could live in such an extreme environment—and it is in these extreme places where they can be found today.

Many, but not all, extremophiles live in anaerobic environments, meaning those without oxygen. Those include tiny pores in rock buried deep in caves; in the darkest, coldest waters of Antarctica; in volcanic vents on the ocean floor; in sulfurous oozing geysers and hot springs; and inside every animal, including humans. At least one species of extremophile has been found "eating" at the wreck of the RMS *Titanic* on the bottom of the Atlantic, creating rust "icicles," or "rusticles," as its waste. Another has been found at a temperature of 250°F (121.1°C). And yet another has come up in a rock core drilled by scientists down to where the Earth is extremely hot, fired by radioactive decay from the planet's core.

EXTREMOPHILES: WHAT THEY ARE

These creatures are called the Archaea, since they are the most ancient life-form of all. They are the trunk of the tree of life itself, from which all other species eventually evolved, including the bacteria.

Scientists studying extremophiles are within fields of science that range from geology to soil science, medicine to astrobiology. So far, some of these tiny life-forms have already been used in medicines. Others are being sought elsewhere in the solar system and probably will have been found on Mars or Titan by the time you hold this book in your hands. Depending upon the species studied, they can also be called thermophiles, hyperthermophiles, acidophiles, alkaliphiles, and other variants. This area of research has plenty of room for scientists of the future.

Scientists agree that extremophiles are not likely to be dangerous to humans. The reason is that they evolved before there was any advantage to being the sort of creature that would eat or even inhabit humans. There were none of us around—and there would not be for another few billion years.

EXTREMOPHILES: MAMMOTH CAVE

Scientists have not yet thoroughly investigated whether extremophiles live in Mammoth Cave. In its areas explored so far, the environment is not particularly extreme. Efforts have not yet been made to burrow deep, searching for those creatures that might live in low-carbon or sulfur-rich environments. It is known, however, that sulfur-consuming extremophiles

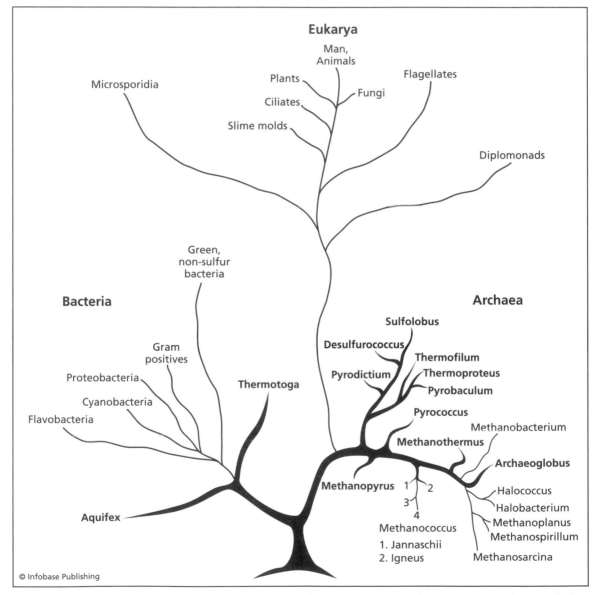

The chart shows in boldface the Archaea, the ancient family of extremophiles. They are lower on the tree of life, which indicates that they are older than even the bacteria and much older than the plants and animals.

exist in Parker's Cave about 15 miles (24 km) away. There, seepage of oil and natural gas has set the stage for them as will be described in chapter 7, on Carlsbad Caverns of New Mexico, where this process exists. (For more on extremophiles, please see chapter sections with their name in other chapters of the book.)

IN THE FIELD: CAVE DATES

Geologists have compared sediments at one level of Mammoth Cave with those in six caves of nearby southern Indiana. They dated both at about 2.6 million years old.

Cave dating of limestone caves was accomplished in two main ways. First, the scientists reconstructed when the Ohio River and its tributaries were rerouted during the Pleistocene. (This happened because of the floods of glacial meltwater, the dates of which are known from other research.)

The dating was also done by analyzing the magnetic polarity of the rock samples: which way was north and which was south in the fossilized magnetic rocks. When rocks that are magnetic (containing iron) solidify, they "freeze" the magnetic pattern that the whole planet had at that time. Our planet has flipped its polarity periodically throughout history—shifted as though the whole Earth were a bar magnet that changed its ends from north to south and south to north. (This happens because of large-scale seething of liquid rock in the *mantle*.) Every rock on the planet follows the lead of the Earth's core at the time that rock solidifies, and some of these rocks have enough magnetism that their north-south orientation can be measured—and, hence, dated. This magnetic polarity phenomenon has proved quite convenient in the dating of caves.

CONSERVATION ISSUES

In karst terrain, aquifers in the area, which are often used as a source of community drinking water, can become polluted, simply because the "pipeline" down to the aquifer is so efficient. Contaminated water seeps down the sinkholes and into the surrounding porous ground and cave cracks. It can then make its way over hundreds of yards, even miles into a city's water supply. Some pollutants are filtered out by the soil or enter storage in area caves, but not nearly all of them.

Karst can also be easily damaged by human construction projects. Plans have been drawn for a 4,000-acre (1,619-ha) industrial park and airport only about six miles (9.65 km) from Mammoth Cave. And other, more recent, plans are for the construction of a large coal-fired power plant some 50 miles (80.5 km) from Mammoth Cave. In this latter case, the major pollutant is mercury, released into the air; particles in the air then come down with the rain.

Mammoth Cave is also threatened by its very success. Visitors not only sometimes litter and damage speleothems (even with oils from their hands), but they also shed barrels of lint from their clothing and even housefuls of skin cells from their bodies. A cave is a nearly closed system, and this material is difficult to vacuum. Some observers think that the cave's cafeteria should be closed, since tiny food particles are also hard to remove.

Progress has been made on two fronts: Kerosene lanterns, once allowed here (and in many other caves) are no longer permitted. Their fumes blacken the rock. And one tour, a boat trip across a Mammoth Cave lagoon, has been halted to avoid harm to the cave shrimp and other creatures.

EARTHQUAKE: 1811–1812

A powerful earthquake shook the Mammoth Cave area from December 16, 1811, to March 5, 1812. Smaller aftershocks lasted on and off for a year afterward.

This "New Madrid earthquake" disrupted the underground mining of saltpeter (a constituent of gunpowder) and the dozens of miners employed there. No one was hurt, but some large boulders were shaken loose from cliffs inside the cave.

The Mammoth Cave area aboveground was lightly populated in those days, unlike today. Geologists differ on future earthquake danger from the fault responsible for this quake. Earthquakes are not a serious problem in the United States' interior, though they do occur.

Mammoth Cave, surely the most famous cave in the United States, is also the cave in the world with the longest total length of its passageways. Like all limestone caves, it was formed by dripping water over millions of years.

2

Cenotes, Chicxulub, and the Caves of Yucatán

Mexico

From an aircraft, the limestone caves of the Yucatán look like green eyes staring out from the face of the green jungle, punching holes in the landscape. Most are not visible except from an airplane or after traversing dense tropical forests of palm, oak, vines, and various flowering trees—for several hours up to several days, in an area of few roads, with a guide. The caves that are open to the sky in this way once had roofs, which collapsed. Others now enclosed will do so, too, eventually. These unusual caves have a link to the death of the dinosaurs, as will emerge in this chapter in connection with Chicxulub.

Called cenotes here (and throughout Central America), these caves capture the rainfall from tropical storms and hold it in underground storage during the dry season, which lasts several months out of the year. The Yucatán—a Mexican province of approximately 135,135 square miles (350,000 km²)—has no rivers running on its surface. Only the cenotes hold the water and feed some of it into the Gulf of Mexico through connections among them. The Yucatán Peninsula from the air and a view of a cenote in the jungle can be seen in the color inserts on page C-2.

The cenotes form a vast system in the Yucatán. Sometimes several of the caves are found in a single .4-square-mile (1-km²) area, sometimes just one lies within an area of several square miles of jungle. Many of them are known to be linked by natural underground tunnels, and miles and miles of passages are still unexplored, making even more linkages possible. The cenotes are like a wet basement under a hot limestone floor, with huge pools of freshwater often evident. Even more water is stored in the pore spaces of the limestone.

The best estimates are that there are about 2,500 cenotes in the Yucatán area alone. Some are quite deep, requiring dives underwater to reach them, and can hold records as the deepest underwater caves in the world (though not the deepest caves overall). Rope ladders or rap-pelling equipment can lead visitors down a 60–200 foot (20–60 m) drop to the water level. Some have walls that ooze acid. Most have several entrances, with the top level usually no more than 30 feet (9 m) below the water's surface. Others hold world records as the longest underwater caves (though, again, not the longest caves overall).

CENOTES SECRET

The names of the cenotes are rarely revealed by the people who live in the area, and their locations are often also kept secret from most non-scientist visitors. (It is easy to lose one's way in this jungle looking for them.) Several do have common names, however. One is called Actún Tunichil Muknal ("Cave of the Stone Sepulchre"). Another, Actún Kava, is 2,442 feet (744 m) long. Yet another, nicknamed "Jaguar Cave" by American explorers, has an entrance of thick calcite columns, with its main passageway 100 feet (30.5 m) wide and 30 feet (9 m) tall. Two to three feet (1 m) of water covers most of Jaguar Cave's floor, and in one area, a pit drops 500 feet (152 m) down. Still another cave, Mil Columnas, meaning 1,000 columns, has many *stalagtites*, along with an altar. And yet another holds the chamber Grutas de Xtacumbilxunaan 450 feet (137 m) below the surface. *Grutas* means *grotto*, another word for cave.

One cenote, indeed well known by its name, is quite famous in an-thropology: Chichen Itza. This cave was the site of ancient human sacri-fice. At least 120 human skeletons, many of them of young women and children, along with much valuable gold and jade, have been found deep within it. Many other cenotes are home to valuable ancient artifacts, too, along with smaller groupings of skeletons.

The Yucatán was—and is—home to the Mayan people. This is a proud and distinguished ancient civilization, whose people built cities that had as many as 90,000 people, during the Classic Mayan era of 250–900 C.E. Their achievements in pyramid-building rivaled those of ancient Egypt. Now, the approximately 7.5 million Maya live here and in other areas of Mexico.

IMPORTANT TO MAYAN CULTURE

The Maya keep many of their cenotes secret today since these sites are still very important to their culture. As mentioned, the caves have both a religious and a domestic use. Cenotes are considered the sacred opening to the underworld Xibalba in the Mayan religion and home to the ruler of that heaven, the god Chac. Sacrifices made to him were done for several reasons, including to end long dry seasons that threatened—and may well have once destroyed—the classic phase of their civilization. Today, the

CENOTES: BEWARE

Surrounded by jungle, the entrances of cenotes are often home to poisonous snakes, killer bee colonies, hornets, thorns and trees that can blister skin, crocodiles, and the occasional jaguar. This is after the usual hike or open jeep ride of hours through the jungle just to get to the mouth of the cave. And do not forget that trip down the long rope ladder. (Anyone tempted to enter a cenote that the Maya do not wish entered—not a good idea—should note that the rope ladders may have been suspiciously altered—after their use.)

Swimming in the cenotes, by permission, of course, introduces a few other considerations. It is indeed possible to wade, swim, or scuba dive in various cenotes. Typically, serious cave divers strap their air tanks to their sides, the better to fit through tight passageways, and take care that the tank is not damaged or even scraped off in these narrow areas. Many people, of course, choose to scuba dive only in the open pits. That way, they can have a wonderful experience—and surface when they want.

Even in open areas, though, divers who go deep can encounter the foggy *halocline*. Here it is hard to see and easy to become disoriented. One's vision can also become impaired or distorted when bubbles breathed out by scuba divers often stir up the silt on the walls or ceilings of a passageway.

The world record for an underwater cave dive now stands at about 1,000 feet (305 m). This is dangerous even for specially certified cave divers, since below 600 feet (183 m) it is possible to get HPNS (high-pressure nervous syndrome). In that condition, one's eyes are compressed, which makes flashing lights appear that are not actually present. It then progresses into tremors, convulsions, and even death. Another depth danger is compression arthralgia. In this condition, one's joints freeze, which makes swimming out difficult or even impossible.

One cenote, Cueva de Villa Luz, in the province of Tabasco, is known for its poisonous levels of hydrogen sulfide gas, toothpaste-like gypsum oozing out from some of its passageway walls, layers of sulfur on other walls, formaldehyde fumes, carbon monoxide, carbon dioxide, small light-pink fish, and probably methane—and the *extremophile* colonies which form the ecosystem partly responsible for these features. A good amount of the toxic chemistry in this cave also comes from the deep springs feeding the cave (they seem to emerge from an oil field in the area). Gas masks are required for cave explorers who plan to scuba dive here.

Blobby white strings composed of some extremophile species in the cenotes have been given a nickname not on the standard list of speleothems: "snottites." They are highly acidic.

---

cenotes are a water source for the Maya. Wooden ladders dangling often 100 feet (30.5 m) down allow them to bring up fresh water in buckets. (Interestingly, the city of Springfield, Missouri, has a related situation. They allow floodwater to flow naturally into the city's 250-some sinkholes and some caves, to prevent flooding at the surface.)

COLLAPSE SINKHOLES

The cenotes are a type of cave called a collapse sinkhole. Similar formations bear the colorful names "banana holes" in Jamaica and "blue holes" in the Bahamas, where they can lie more than 200 feet (61 m) below the ocean surface. Florida has quite a few sinkholes, with a dramatic one opening in January 2005. At 225 feet (69 m) wide and 50 feet (15 m) deep, it opened suddenly after hurricane rains had saturated the soils. This sinkhole swallowed trees, road signs, utility poles, and a section of a street, snarling traffic. It took nearly 1,300 dump-truck loads of sand to fill it in.

Collapsing sinkholes—as opposed to those that more often keep their "roofs"—occur most often in humid areas such as Mexico's Tropics. Lots of rainfall occur in this area, in season, and there is no freezing season at all. This means lots of mildly acidic water dripping down into the limestone. There it dissolves the rock away steadily, all year long.

Mexico, a tropical country, features cenotes, and the limestone terrain in which they form, over broad areas beyond even the Yucatán. Provinces such as Oaxaca, Guarero, Queretaro, San Luis Potosi, Puebla, Tabasco, Tamaulipas, Chiapas, and Santa Cruz—nine out of the country's 31 states—are also home to these karst caves.

A major collapse sinkhole is Dos Ojos, meaning "two eyes." It is one of the largest, available for visitors' exploration, and has features such as stalactites from which water drips as far as 12–15 feet (4.5 m) down to the floor. The cenote Balankanche also has a tour available to the public.

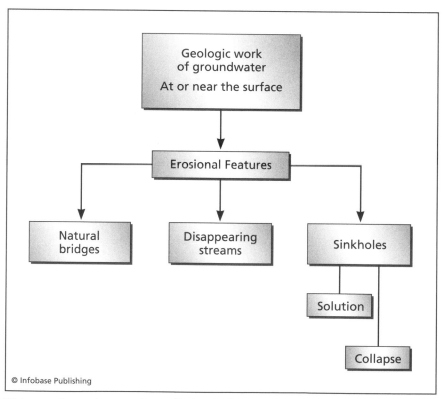

© Infobase Publishing

Water moving underground, usually just in drips, creates all these features over long periods of time.

FORMATION: WATER TABLE LOCATION

The cenotes all formed at or below the *water table*, which is typical for limestone caves. Since they are still wet, they are likely to be growing more today. This is certainly not always the case with limestone caves. This type of cave begins to form as water—mildly acidic because it contains runoff from soils at the surface—drips down through the tiny pores and cracks that exist naturally in the rock.

Limestone typically has three kinds of such cracks. The first are called the "partings," opening parallel to the rock's natural (horizontal) layers. Next are the "joints," which cut across the horizontal layers and are caused mostly by "Earth tides." These are the small, twice-daily, flexing movements of the solid Earth caused by the Moon's gravity, and they gradually weaken the rock. (The Moon moves water much more easily than land, creating the ocean tides.) The third type of crack is the "faults," which cut across in areas where the rock layers have been displaced; these broader rock movements are caused by *plate tectonics*.

The water proceeds through these three kinds of cracks, or channels, down toward the water table, slowly and gradually dissolving a bit of the limestone rock on the way. Over time, some of the cracks become enlarged. When a water channel becomes about .2 inch (5 cm) in diameter, it becomes its most efficient at dissolving the rock. Geologists think the reason for this is that, at that diameter, the water becomes turbulent within its tube. This churning, swirling turbulence creates more contact between the water and the surface of the rock. (Scientists in various fields study turbulence quite a bit, in everything from the atmosphere to river flow to the circulation of galaxies; it is a concept that goes well beyond cave water.)

As water from the surface reaches the water table, through all the kinds of cracks available, the mildly acidic water then is in permanent contact with the rock. This is the wet zone. Down here, also, there is plenty of carbon dioxide, and it mixes with the calcite in the rock there, which is especially soluble. This is why a wet cave such as a cenote is probably still forming, growing.

WATER STORAGE/LAYERS

The cenotes are among the wettest grouping of caves on the planet. Across the Earth, groundwater represents only about six-tenths of 1 percent of all the freshwater—but that adds up to about 960,000 cubic miles (4 million km³) of water. (This places groundwater second only to the glaciers as freshwater storage places. They hold about six times as much as groundwater does. Lakes come in third.)

In addition to freshwater, the cenotes contain some saltwater from the ocean. This is true even if a particular cave is far from the ocean, since the Yucatán underground is a honeycomb of caves. Underground passages lead ultimately to the sea on both the east and west coasts of the province.

If both exist in a cenote, the freshwater and saltwater form separate horizontal layers. (This is fortunate for those using the cenotes for drinking water.) The thinner, mixing layer between them is the halocline, a zone that appears murky and was mentioned earlier in connection with the hazard it can present to cavers.

Typically, the top freshwater layer is home to some fish. The second, purplish, halocline layer has some specialized bacteria. The third layer down is brown and rich in hydrogen sulfide, with some insect larvae and oozing, thick, white strands of sulfur bacteria. (These will be discussed further in the section on the extremophiles.) And, on the bottom, the clear saltwater layer has cave fish and shrimp, both blind. Of course, not every cenote is situated properly or is deep enough to have all these layers.

FORMATION: GIANT METEORITE HIT

The cenotes, a massive cave system, formed not only because of the limestone, though that was required—and not only because the tropical climate provided plenty of water seepage. The rock of this province has an exceptionally large number of cracks, making for plenty of downward, narrow water routes. The reason for these cracks: A giant meteor smashed down here. The impact of it not only kicked up enough rock, ocean water, and general debris to darken the sky for months, but it stressed the rock in an extreme fashion and over a considerable period of time.

This meteor, scientists believe, is the very one to have caused the extinction of the dinosaurs and much of the rest of life on Earth at the time, about 65 million years ago. It was probably about six miles (10 km) across and blazed down at about 20 miles (32 km) per second. This massive object hit the Yucatán with immense force, punching about 2.5 miles (4 km) down into solid ground. This impact first created a crater 110 miles (177 km) across. Then, as the crater walls collapsed and powerful shockwaves moved outward, a larger crater formed, about 150 miles (241 km) in diameter. A ring of new islands was also created, visible after the resulting tsunami receded. No humans were here to experience this. But everything alive on Earth at the that time suffered.

The impact's center is near the town of Chicxulub, in the northwestern part of the Yucatán Peninsula. And the whole Yucatán landmass was changed, setting the stage for the cenotes seen today.

The three-dimensional jigsaw puzzle of cracks in the Earth that led to the cenotes did not form in the first few days after the meteorite hit—and neither did the death scenario of the dinosaurs and most other creatures unfold in an instant. Initially, pulverized rock, soils, and vaporized water hurtled into the atmosphere. They blocked the Sun, causing the plants and small creatures that eat them to die. The dinosaurs died later, when they, too, had nothing to eat, not even each other. Stress on the rocks gradually fractured them over a period of several million years. And the sea creatures that survived the catastrophe also gradually added their shells and skeletons until thick limestone layers had formed on the seafloor. As these compacted, the bowl of the meteorite crater gradually filled. Then, about 50 million years ago, the limestone was uplifted in plate tectonic processes, further stressing the rock. The shape of the crater wall reemerged, now vague with age but still detectable in aerial photographs today. Most of the impacted rock, though, is now buried under several hundred meters of sediment.

The ring of cenotes around Chicxulub, on land and continuing underwater out to sea, formed above two of the concentric rims of the ancient crater, following its every outline. They do so today. And the shape of the crater wall directed the drainage system through all the cenotes of the Yucatán. It still does so today. In a way, it was an immense trade: dinosaurs for cenotes.

The circle around the town of Chicxulub shows the large area of the ancient meteorite's impact.

ENVIRONMENTAL ISSUES

In an area as riddled with connected caves as the Yucatán, pollutants entering the groundwater find their way to the water in other caves. Drinking water can be contaminated by sewage, even that disposed of dozens of miles away. Though this is true in all karst terrains, it is especially so here since hundreds and hundreds of the cenotes are connected, invisibly, underground.

This amazing area is also feeling the pressure of tourism. About 10,000 visitors scuba in the cenotes each year, and not all of them are careful with the caves' formations. Some of the cenotes have become privately owned ecoareas.

Speleothems

Speleothems, or cave decorations, such as stalactites, stalagmites, and soda straws, are indeed present in the cenotes. (Please see chapter 1, on the Mammoth Cave of Kentucky, for how these form.) Since these are made by dripping water, the speleothems were created on the cave floor and ceiling when it was dry or nearly so. Dripstone features, once about the water level, including some large stalagmites, are now underwater in some of the caves and have been so for about 10,000 years. They have stopped growing but are sturdy enough not to wash away. Visitors can swim among them in cavern chambers. Some of these formations are white, mottled yellow, and even orange, depending upon their mineral content.

All these cenote speleothems were created during the *Pleistocene*, when the land here was dry. (The glaciers had "locked up" so much water that the sea level fell.) In fact, Ice Age mammal bones are sometimes found among them.

One interesting formation, called shelfstone, can be seen in some of the cenotes. It begins as a thin scum on the water, building up through mineral and even bacterial deposits. Then the thickening mat glues itself to a wall until it is as thick as perhaps 10 feet (3 m). When the water receded (during a cold period of the Pleistocene), these shelfstones emerged as actual shelves attached to the cave wall. Many of them are strong enough to walk on today.

EXTREMOPHILES

This highly unusual group of creatures is the focus of a new area of scientific research here and elsewhere. Three new biologic "kingdoms" of them have been found in caves in just the last five or six years. (See chapter 1 as well as other sections for more material on them.) In fact, both the biological component of the shelfstone formation and the oozing walls mentioned earlier in this chapter are probably partly or wholly composed of extremophiles.

When scientists observe formations that appear to have crystals of the mineral calcium carbonate formed around an organic bit of bacteria or yeast, they are increasingly testing for the presence of these hardy microscopic life-forms. Sometimes called bacteria in popular magazines, extremophiles are neither bacteria nor yeast. They are even more ancient and at least as strangely varied.

In one cenote in the province of Tabasco, a slimy white extremophile has been found that eats sulfur and excretes a sulfuric acid stronger than battery acid. This coats the cave walls and ceilings. In fact, scientists have discovered that a lot of the hyperthermophiles (the name for the heat-

EL SÓTANO

This cenote, in the province in Queretaro, is an 11-hour hike from the village of Ayutla, lying within thick jungle. The cenote's immense depth—fourth on the world-record list of vertical *pits* within caves—has attracted small groups of adventurous cavers who have measured its depth: 1,194 feet (364 m). It is also the third most voluminous cave in the world, with a water volume of 21 million cubic yards (16 million m[3]).

The following is a list of the 21 caves with the deepest drops—without any usable ledges on the way down, or up:

Höllenhöhle	Austria	1,476 feet	(450 m)
Minye	Papua New Guinea	1,368 feet	(417 m)
Provatina	Greece	1,276 feet	(389 m)
El Sótano	Mexico	1,194 feet	(364 m)
Stierwascherschacht	Austria	1,148 feet	(350 m)
sima Aonda	Venezuela	1,148 feet	(350 m)
Mavro Skiadi	Greece	1,122 feet	(342 m)
Las Golondrinas	Mexico	1,093/1,234 feet	(333/376 m)[1]
Tomasa Kiahua	Mexico	1,083 feet	(330 m)
Aphanize	France	1,076 feet	(328 m)[2]
Lépineaux	Spain	1,050 feet	(320 m)
Nare	Papua New Guinea	1,017 feet	(310 m)
pozzo Mandini	Italy	1,017 feet	(310 m)
Xonga	Mexico	1,017 feet	(310 m)
Vicente Alegre	Spain	1,014 feet	(309 m)
Altes Murmeltier	Austria	1,007 feet	(307 m)
Pozo Trasla Jayada	Spain	1,004 feet	(306 m)
Pot II	France	991 feet	(302 m)
Touya de Liet	France	991 feet	(302 m)
Juhué	Spain	991 feet	(302 m)
Enrico Revel	Italy	981/1,037 feet	(299/316 m)[1]

[1]Depending on the reference point chosen
[2]Ascending section not explored
Source: *Atlas of the Great Caves of the World*

loving extremophiles) live on sulfur. Extremophiles have also been found in the haloclines of cenotes, and these are known as the halophiles (salt-loving). Of the 50-some such species identified worldwide—so far—some live in the Great Salt Lake, Death Valley, the Dead Sea, and salty lakes in Antarctica.

IN THE FIELD: ANCIENT CLIMATE CLUES

The cenotes are the focus of much research. This ranges from archaeological and anthropological efforts to understand both ancient and contemporary Mayan culture to hydrology attempts to use the cenotes even more fully for water storage. It includes the use of dye traces to establish more connections among the cenotes (colored dye is released in one cave and evidence of that colored water sought in others), and it focuses on the extremophiles mentioned earlier in the chapter.

Cenote research also leads to insights into ancient climate, and this involves several approaches. Animal bones collected, especially those of a huge armadillo and a horse species now extinct, show that the Yucatán was once a vast, dry grassland. (That is the environment in which creatures like these are known to live.)

The speleothems here can even be used to help date the pulses of glaciation, though no glacier ever reached even close to this far south. Cave deposits can show when the water table was lower—when glaciers locked up enough water, as snowfall, the oceans fell. During these times, the speleothems grew, requiring, as they do, dry conditions. As glaciers melted worldwide, oceans rose, drowning the growth process of the speleothems. Their layers can be "read" similar to the way tree rings are read.

Stalagmites can even be used to find evidence of hurricane periods. In a hurricane, it rains "lighter" rain rather than heavier rain. Different isotopes (chemical versions) of oxygen exist in nature in general. Hurricanes feature fierce winds, which cause a lot of evaporation in the swirls of air they contain. After awhile, a hurricane's rain becomes filled with more of the lighter isotopes of oxygen. A study of the oxygen isotope layers in a stalagmite can detect times when the climate was more fraught with these violent storms.

The cenote caves of the Yucatán are known for their extensive underground network. The origin of this system lies in an ancient hit by a meteorite.

3

Lascaux Cave of Southwestern France

This cave in southwestern France was discovered by four teenagers. Stories conflict as to how exactly this happened. One of the young men might have first seen his dog's head and shoulders disappear for a moment down a hole in the ground, to chase a ball, then decided to look down himself. Or, the four might all have been searching for a rumored underground passageway, supposed to lead to a local manor house where a treasure was believed hidden.

It is known definitely, though, that these teenagers were walking in the woods a mile or so outside their town of Montignac, France, and somehow noticed a hole in the ground surrounded by tree roots. They peered down—then decided to really investigate. Returning the next day with a light, rope, and knife, they dug out the hole until it was big enough to climb into, feet first, one person at a time. What they saw amazed them, even though they had no idea—yet—that they were the first to see this cave in 5,000 years. After a few days of trying to keep the place as their secret, they decided to invite one of their teachers down for a look. The year was 1940. The rest, as the expression goes, is history.

Lascaux could well be the most famous cave in the world, certainly the most famous in Europe. Like other limestone caves, it is a bit of a maze, chambers connected by passageways, zigzagging to lower and lower levels. Though its formation will be described later in the chapter, this architecture is not unusual either. It does not even have the most *speleothems*, formations such as stalactites and stalagmites. And it is not actually unique in its cave art either—that is found in more than 200 other caves in Europe, with variants elsewhere.

Lascaux's fame is because it is home to the most elaborate, amazing, mysterious, and beautiful cave art in the world, paintings on and carvings into the cave's walls and roof by Cro-Magnon hunters and gatherers. These were Ice Age people, living here south of the glacier in the land of mammoths, giant wild bulls, and primitive wild horses. They, like many of the animals who shared their world, are now extinct (though, in a sense, the Cro-Magnons became modern Europeans). They created here about 1,700 painting and engravings, and a re-creation of part of this activity is seen in the color insert on page C-3.

CRO-MAGNONS IN CAVES

These people of the Ice Age first arrived in France about 40,000 years ago, a new stage of habitation in an area that had been home to more primitive peoples for about 400,000 years. The Cro-Magnons were not the terrifying, hairy brutes constantly hitting each other over the head with rocks that one might imagine from television cartoons, though they were indeed "Stone Age," or Paleolithic, people. This is the name for the phase of human culture when tools were made of stone, wood, and other found materials; metals such as bronze had not yet been exploited.

But their culture had sophistication. They used fire for light, understood both weaponry and cooking, spoke a language now unknown to us, and were acquainted with the Milky Way, Moon, and constellations as direction-finders. In addition, they made clothes that had buttons and dressed warmly in animal hides in a way similar to today's native Arctic people. Their way of life was built around hunting and gathering their food, since the cultivation of crops—agriculture—was not yet in existence except in East Asia and the Mideast (and not even there until probably 10,000 years ago). They were somewhat shorter and stockier than humans today, but they looked nothing like gorillas or chimpanzees. They looked more like us than they did the Neanderthal people, who died out at about this same time, approximately 35,000–30,000 years ago, replaced by these more advanced Cro-Magnons.

These Cro-Magnons were also gifted artists, at least in the period from 15,000 to 9,000 B.C.E. This most prolific era, their renaissance, is called the Magdalenian period. Limestone caves were their galleries. And, like us today, some of them were better artists than others. Differences in artistry can be seen even within Lascaux.

These Ice Age people did not live deep in the caves and did not always inhabit the caves at all. When they did use them for shelter, they lived in the front sections in view of the sunlight. It was convenient: Here in the Dordogne River valley alone, dozens of caves bite into the limestone. Some of the names now are Tuc d'Audoubert, Gargos, Rouffignac Niaux, and Cougnac, and all show fossil or artistic evidence from the Cro-Magnon era. (The reason for the large numbers of caves in this area will be described later in the chapter.)

Shelter was important to the Cro-Magnons because it was cold during their time on Earth. Glaciers blanketed Scandinavia to the north and extended as far down as about 55°N latitude, that of Dresden, Germany (and even farther south at high elevations such as in the Alps). But life was not unbearable. Herds of reindeer, bison, and other large animals were plentiful, as were fish, clams, and seasonal berries and nuts. The climate was quite stable, at least in their heyday, beginning about 15,000 B.C.E. This created less stress for survival.

PAINTS FROM MINERALS

Cro-Magnons had enough leisure time to make paints, using the minerals of the Earth. Two types of iron-rich soils, ochre and hematite, were used to make red, yellow, and brown. The soils were held together with water, animal fat, and perhaps the whites of birds' eggs. Black paint and violet paint were made from two different forms of manganese, another mineral, and some of the dark black came from charcoal. They mixed their paints to get varying shades and combinations, creating subtle shadings. They may have created other colors, too, but, if so, these have faded and are no longer visible. As shall be described in one of the "In the Field" sections, scientists have been able to date their artwork partly by analyzing the paints.

(Other geologists have used cave sediments at Lascaux to study climate history, since caves are like basement storage spaces. In them are preserved pollen layers that were blown or tracked in, and the kinds of pollen reflect what was growing outside. Scientists who study evidence like this are called geoarchaeologists.)

To apply the paint to the cave, these Stone Age artists used sticks, reeds, hair, bits of moss and animal fur, hollow bone tubes, stone scrapers, and probably other techniques and tools that have not left a record. The Cro-Magnons also built wooden scaffolding, held together with rope (from the sinews of animals). This allowed them to paint high on the walls and the ceiling of the cave (where most of their art, in fact, is found). Since they chose to work deep in the cave, they also made stone bowls into lamps by filling them with animal fat and burning it. They also had wooden torches. Since Lascaux lay so undisturbed for so long, these objects have been found in significant numbers—even some of their ancient "paint palettes" of flat bone lie on the floor. Popped-off buttons from their clothing have also been located and studied.

The Cro-Magnons worked right through a barbeque lunch or dinner. Scientists have found the bones of reindeer, red deer, and ibex (a wild goat) on the floor under the artwork—with human tooth marks in them. Their footprints also have been preserved in this amazing limestone cave, along with some of their handprints on the wall.

What these people created is elaborate and complex enough to indicate a new and richer stage of human development than had been known so far. Their minds and imaginations were in the same league as humans' today.

LIMESTONE CAVE PAINTING AND CARVING

Like all large limestone caves, this one has intersecting chambers and passageways. In Lascaux, seven different areas were used by the Cro-Magnon artists. They are now called the Hall of the Bulls, the Axial Gallery, the Passageway, the Nave, the Well, the Chamber of the Felines, and the Shaft. In many cases, the artists used the cave's natural lines, ridges, bumps, and slopes as part of their art—red deer "swim" along a raised, wavy line in the limestone, for example, their heads as if above water. And horses sometimes leap, as though jumping toward a cave pit. In some cave areas, notably the Hall of Bulls and the Axial Gallery, the limestone had a thin layer of *calcite*, even at the time of their painting. This common cave mineral is formed by dripping water, out of which the mineral *precipitates*. In this chemical condition, paint fuses to the wall very quickly. Though this did not allow the artists to have "rough drafts," it did help to preserve the art. In the Nave, however, the people were able to cut right into the bare, soft limestone. The organic nature of their art followed the organic nature of the cave rock.

What the Cro-Magnons painted, largely animals and with biological accuracy, reveals a lot about this time in the *Pleistocene* or Ice Age. All the animals are wild, and some are huge. The Hall of Bulls pictures four large creatures called aurochs, a bull-like animal now extinct. They are shown as 10–16 feet (3–5 m) long, not much bigger than their actual size as seen in fossilized bones. The hall also depicts wild cows, deer, horses, and a bear. The Cro-Magnon people had not yet domesticated any animals, with the possible exception of wolves into dogs (though that is not known from the paintings).

The Axial Gallery has horses, more aurochs and cows, extinct bison, deer, and ibex (a wild goat, now rare but not extinct). The Nave is filled with horses, some with lines near them that look like arrows, and also features some bison. In the lowest area of the cave, 16 feet (5 m) below the other levels and the oldest section, is the place called the Shaft. Deep down here is the cave's only image of a person, a man leaning in front of a bison. In a way, Lascaux Cave is alive with dead animals and long-gone human beings.

WHY THOSE ANIMALS?

Scientists wonder about the culture of these people. Why did they paint almost no reindeer, which was their main animal food, along with mammoths, which they also hunted regularly, while they did use the caves to depict many horses and bison, consumed to a lesser extent? Why did they never paint salmon, clams, and the small birds which they are also known to have eaten?

Ponder this: Our culture has not named sports team, or much else, after the familiar hamburger, chicken, steak, and seafood either. And animals such as eagles, lions, and tigers are viewed in our art far more than say, squirrels and pigeons, which are much more common. Ties between people and the animal world have always been strong—and still are. Maybe the Cro-Magnons, like us, identified with the greater grandeur of the creatures they painted. No one is sure. (An example of one of their large and impressive paintings is found in the color insert on page C-3.)

An old theory about Lascaux Cave focuses on "hunting magic" to explain its nature. It suggested that the Cro-Magnons painted the animals they wished to hunt successfully, something like doing a rain dance to pray for rainfall. This theory is no longer particularly popular.

Other theories no longer as widely held suggest that the cave was a site for some sort of initiation of teenagers into adulthood, or that the animals were the gods of the Cro-Magnons (especially the ones painted on the ceiling). More recent thinking is that their religious leader, called the shaman, might have seen these animals when entering a trance, or that the tribe was story-telling, or that they simply loved the animals and loved to make art depicting them. No one will ever know. And there may be many reasons for the creation of an amazing cave display like Lascaux.

Three things are particularly mysterious. Why is only one animal in this cave an unreal one? A creature with two thin horns and circular patches has not been identified with any real Ice Age animal, anywhere. There are also colored squares and lines of dots within some of the paintings and carvings, and these more abstract symbols have not been deciphered. Then there is the strangest fact of all: Why did the Cro-Magnon people abandon Lascaux about 8,000 years ago, never to return. Was it the stress on their culture as the world warmed, causing animal extinctions and the movement to the north of other species? Did they overhunt, killing too many? Again, we will never know.

MANY CAVES AROUND HERE

France and Spain are rich in caves. France, home to Lascaux, has caves in every county (called a *departement*). Nearly 200 of them are more than 100 feet (30 m) deep, more than 1.85 miles (3 km) long, or both. Two of these caves—réseau Jean Bernard, at 5,036 feet (1,535 m) deep, and réseau de la Pierre Saint-Martin, at 4,403 feet (1,342 m)—are among the deepest caves in the world. The caves in France and Spain are also notably long. Spain's Altamira Cave is also second only to Lascaux in the splendor of its Paleolithic or Stone Age art. And a cave near Granada, Spain, also with much cave art, has been kept closed to the public for more than 30 years as scientists try to figure out how many people can be admitted, for how long, without damaging the art. The Cro-Magnon imprint and legacy is strong in this part of the world.

The reason for all the caves in this area is the limestone bedrock, called *karst terrain*. Limestone, made primarily of the compacted bodies of tiny sea creatures, long dead, is an especially porous rock. The tiny fractures and joints, usually invisible, become pathways for water dripping down from the surface. Gradually, the drip spaces expand slightly, allowing yet more water to seep down. Because the water begins as rain hitting the sur-

France and Spain are home to hundreds of caves.

face, it brings down with it chemicals from the soils and decaying plants at the surface. These chemicals make the water acidic—very slightly, nothing like the acidity of a soft drink, for example—but acidic enough for the water to be able to chemically dissolve the soft limestone rock.

As cave building continues, chambers and passageways grow, along with the vertical drip waterways hidden in the rocks. Sometimes water also enters the cave with more force and volume—in a stream or perhaps even a river. But this does not necessarily happen. Limestone caves are made by far more drips than by visibly flowing water.

Areas such as the Dordogne River valley here, now inland, were once under the sea. (Hence the fossilized sea creatures that compose the limestone.) In times of ancient glaciation, much ocean water was tied up as ice; so sea levels were lower. Melting glaciers raised the levels again. Like a seesaw, the Lascaux area was alternately coastline, inland, under the sea, and now, inland again.

Limestone-rich areas, the karst terrain of the planet, are often found near the current edges of the continents for this reason (though they can be found anywhere that fractured limestone bedrock exists).

EXTREMOPHILES

Limestone caves, as well as other environments that might seem a difficult place for organisms to live, can be home to extremophiles. These are creatures more ancient than any primitive bacteria ever found. (For more about them, see chapter 1 as well as other sections that mention extremophiles in their titles.) Geomicrobiologists have found them in the rock art caves of Europe and studied them with *mass spectroscopy*, a technique described in the "In the Field" section later in the chapter.

Extremophiles grow in near-invisible colonies. When their numbers become large enough, they are more easily detectable as a *biofilm*, a living (or sometimes fossilized) layer that forms on cave surfaces. The chemistry of this biofilm allows other minerals to build up on the cave. The process can even change the color of paint. And limestone and marble seem especially affected.

Once thought to be merely a natural, chemical process acting on old rock, perhaps from dust or soot, these mineral changes on cave surfaces are now known to be biologically induced—by extremophiles, usually.

AFTER THE CRO-MAGNONS: US

Lascaux Cave slept, hiding its cave walls and preserving its art, which ranges from as old as 17,000 years to as recent as about 9,000 years. At some point, probably about 8,000 years ago, ground-shifting and surface water flow moved, collapsed, and closed off most of the opening. Only the small hole was left to be discovered later, much later, by the four teenagers.

The cave was opened to the public in 1948 and soon attracted hundreds of visitors a day. People were astounded, as were the scientists who made it a subject of their research.

Quite soon, though, visitors were noticing headaches. They were breathing up much of Lascaux's oxygen (creating the headaches when it ran a bit low). They were also exhaling carbon dioxide, water vapor, and even body heat. One person, in one hour, breathes out 21–29 quarts (20–25 L) of carbon dioxide, about one ounce of water, and emits the heat of an 82–116 watt lightbulb. The chemistry of the cave was changing. Water vapor, condensing on the walls, became droplets, dripping down more and more often through the art. The French government installed a ventilation system that did help.

CAVE RE-CREATION AND MORE CAVE ART

Because Lascaux had to be closed to the public—at a time when its popularity was immense and unlikely to diminish—the French decided to re-create the experience of it for visitors. They built Lascaux II, a cave about 650 feet (200 m) from Lascaux, featuring a complete copy of the Hall of Bulls and the Axial Gallery chambers—though painted in the 1980s. Using the concrete walls of an abandoned quarry, the artist hired for the project made the same mineral paint pigments as the Cro-Magnons had, then created the same animal figures. About 30,000 visitors a year have come to see Lascaux II since it opened in 1983.

Also featuring objects of Ice Age art, but real ones found in yet other area caves, the National Museum of Prehistory, nearby in France's Dordogne Valley, opened in 2004. The artifacts here include a bison carved in bone between 15,000 and 14,000 years ago, stone engravings that date back 30,000 years, and a child's skeleton that dates to 50,000 years ago, all genuine primitive objects.

The Dordogne River valley also features a few additional real caves, small ones, which are open to the public.

Though the Cro-Magnon cave art of Europe is spectacular with its pictured animals, this is not the only place that cave art has been found. Australia has hundreds of thousands of rock drawings from the Ice Age period. Use of ochre for red color dates back to about 43,000 years ago in Africa. And simpler bone, ivory, and stone art—markings that could be countings or calendars—date to much earlier, perhaps even to 300,000 years ago.

Petroglyphs, also called pictographs, are the name for the rock art of the United States. They are often, but not always, found in caves, especially in the desert Southwest. The images are of deer, mountain lions, sheep, bison, and many more human figures than have been found in European Ice Age art. American petroglyphs, in and outside of caves, usually date from a few hundred up to a few thousand years old, though research continues here, and older dates might be established.

Though it may or may not be considered art, human bones have been found decorated for burial, from even more ancient times than the era of cave wall art. Neanderthal bones, the human group who preceded the Cro-Magnons, have been discovered in shallow caves of southern France. Some of them are colored with red ochre, probably a burial ritual. No other art has been found from these more primitive people whose heyday era was between about 150,000 and 30,000 years ago. The Neanderthals disappeared by about 40,000 years ago, replaced by the Cro-Magnons.

Visitor numbers soon doubled. All the extra electric lights to accommodate the visitors added their heat to the mix, and pollen continued to blow in or get tracked into the cave. Green spots and small white blobs began to disfigure the walls. The green turned out to be algae and bacteria, and the white was excess calcite, with extremophiles surely contributing. With great sorrow, the French government closed the cave to the public in 1963. Only a few scientists and writers are now allowed to enter, by permit, and they may stay only a short time.

The cave story in France may not yet all have been written. In 1994, a new network of ancient caves now called Chauvet Cave was discovered (by an adult) in a nearby river valley. The oldest of the 100-some wall paintings here are from 32,000 to 30,000 years ago, even older than the art in Lascaux. The art features leopards, hyenas, owls, and other animals not seen at Lascaux, many painted down to the whisker and with exquisite shading. This cave system will never be opened to the public, in order to preserve it.

Most recently, in the year 2000, yet another grouping of caves was discovered, again in the Dordogne Valley in which Lascaux is located. There are about 100 examples of cave art here, including a bison 12 feet (3.6 m) long. More caves with ancient art probably remain to be discovered here and elsewhere around the world.

IN THE FIELD: CARBON-14 DATING

Geologists drill down into rock and pull cores back up to study the ages of rock layers. But looking at these layers does not yield much insight unless and until geologists can figure out what period of history each slice comes from. They do this through rock dating. One method is called carbon-14 dating.

Carbon-14 dating takes advantage of the fact that nitrogen in the atmosphere is continually blasted with cosmic rays from space—they turn it into a very mildly radioactive form of carbon, called carbon 14. The plants of the planet build up this carbon while they are alive, and some of that remains in their tissues after they die, fossilized. All radioactive elements such as carbon 14 gradually decay, but each at a different rate, and this process has been analyzed. So scientists know that half the carbon 14 in a slice of rock decays every 5,730 years. A half of that half decays in another 5,730 years, and so on. Thus, 5,730 years is called the half-life of the carbon-14 element. This sets up the dating yardstick, and then scientists measure how much carbon-14 is in a layer of the rock core they are studying.

Alert readers will notice that, after awhile, there will not be much, if any, carbon 14 left. And, in fact, this dating method takes scientists back just 40,000 years before it becomes impractical to use. It also does not work at all on rock unless the rock was once a living plant or animal. Materials such as wood, shell, pottery, linen, and pollen can, however, also be dated using this method. So it works well for "recent" history such as the Cro-Magnon period.

Dating at Lascaux has shown quite definitively that the art is at least as old as 10,000 years. Analysis of the natural "varnish" layer (really a biofilm, as described earlier in the chapter) that formed over the paint, and of the biochemistry of the paint material itself, has corroborated these dates.

The Lascaux Cave is known as the most amazing cave in the world for Cro-Magnon or Stone Age art. Perhaps no one will ever know exactly why this array of paintings was created, deep in a cave.

4

Lubang Nasib Bagus and the Sarawak Chamber of Borneo

Malaysia

Near the equator in the South China Sea, southeast of Thailand, southwest of the Philippines, and north of Java lies the large island of Borneo. A broad section of Borneo belongs to the country of Malaysia, and this includes the northern province called Sarawak. Within Sarawak's tropical rain forests, massive amounts of limestone, along with sandstones and shales, form high mountains, valleys, and basins.

Hidden inside and among these mountains lie many large caves. One is called Lubang (also written as Lobang) Nasib Bagus, translated as Good Luck Cave. And within this cave is the Sarawak Chamber. It is the largest cave chamber in the world, a single room far larger than any football "superdome." Some sense of its size can be gleaned in the upper color photo insert on page C-4. The Sarawak Chamber and its broader environs are part of a Malaysian national park.

GUNUNG MULU NATIONAL PARK

Good Luck Cave and its Sarawak Chamber were explored extensively in the early to mid-1980s, and the cave has been within a national park since 1985. The park covers about 210 square miles (545 km²) of northwest Borneo, near the border with Brunei. Inside the park and outside of it, along the Sarawak shoreline and indeed the whole Borneo shoreline, the *terrain* is *karst*, layers of limestone/sandstone/shale rock—cave territory. Most of the caves of Sarawak have been hollowed out of individual hills and are isolated from each other. But here, near Mulu Mountain (*gunung* means mountain in Malay), the caves form a massive interconnected system.

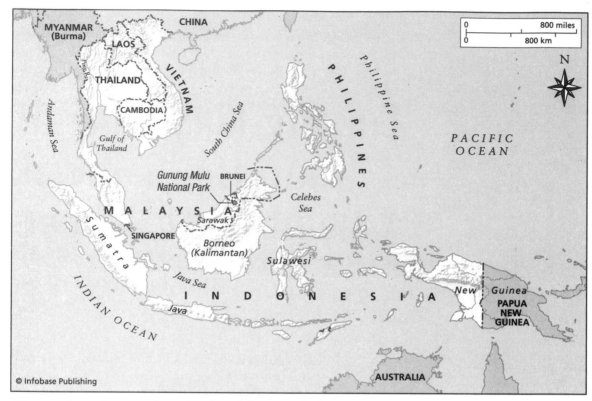

This map shows the approximate location of the Sarawak Chamber which is part of the Gunung Mulu National Park of Malaysia.

Through a 25-mile (40-km) band, caves are common, and more connections among them surely remain to be discovered. The topography, the lay of the land, is what makes the difference here. Rivers such as the Melinau River flow among and down the mountains. They direct the ample rain forest rainfall—about 200 inches (508 cm) a year—to lower areas. There, it can drip through soils composed of the rich tropical vegetation. (As has been described in chapter 1 and chapter 2, limestone caves like Sarawak are made by dripping water, and, to a lesser extent, by flowing water.) Visitors to the Mulu area can see rivers sweeping right into mountains, vanishing from sight amid the humid and incessant dripping of the rain forest.

Malaysians and other geologists believe that many more whole new caves are hidden, remaining to be discovered, in Gunung Mulu National Park and surrounding areas. The density of the rain forest vegetation makes exploration difficult.

HUGE CHAMBER

Good Luck Cave's Sarawak Chamber is likely to remain the prize-winning largest single chamber on the planet. As the most immense natural cave chamber of all, this single "room" is three or four times larger than the largest indoor football stadium ever built, and it could house 40 large Boeing 747 airplanes. Just to cover the length of the Sarawak Chamber would take seven of these giant planes, nose to nose. (Of course, the airplanes could never get through the opening of Good Luck Cave to begin with.)

Sarawak Chamber is more than 2,000 feet (600 m) long, nearly 1,500 feet (457 m) wide, and has a floor surface area of 1.75 million square

This image shows an entrance to the high-ceilinged cave. *(Courtesy of Jerry Wooldridge, photographer)*

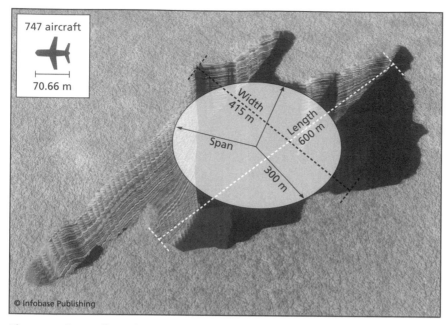

747 aircraft

70.66 m

Width 415 m

Length 600 m

Span

300 m

© Infobase Publishing

The approximate dimensions of the Sarawak Chamber

feet (162,700 m²). Its volume is approximately 425 million cubic feet (12,034,660 m³).

Stalactites and stalagmites are scarcely present in Sarawak Chamber. Instead, giant boulders are tumbled around as though ancient monsters had had a rock fight. Both its size and relative lack of speleothems proceed from the same cause: This chamber is as large as it is because the roofs and walls of various other passageways have collapsed into it. This collapse expanded its original size, which was probably already immense. The collapse also destroyed the cave formations.

Limestone caves do tend to grow and to collapse readily, of course. But here, in the Tropics, rainfall over the eons has been so ample and steady that caves have the potential to grow extremely large. More water means gradually more and larger "dripways" within the rock—the rock becomes almost like locked-in blocks of Swiss cheese. More and more rock is then dissolved to open more and more cave. Here, too, a mountain river flows through the cave, widening the passageways considerably over time. *Tectonic* fault lines exist, too (as shall be described). Also, no glacier extended anywhere near this latitude in at least the last 2 million years of the *Pleistocene;* so water was never tied up as ice to provide a break in the cave's expansion.

The Sarawak Chamber is not open to the public, nor is any part of Good Luck Cave. The chamber itself has not even been completely explored (mostly because of all the boulders). Even the passageway to it is usually filled with water and boulders, and an interior canyon within it also makes exploration a true challenge.

CAVE "MOUTHS" IN MULU

The location of the Gunung Mulu National Park caves near the equator leads to an unusual smaller feature at many of the cave entrances: sharp, greenish, spikey rock masses in which all the spikes point toward the cave entrance. The greenish color comes from cyanobacteria, an ancient form of bacteria that coats the rock, but more unusually, so do the sharp points. These rock points are what is left after the rock became pitted with large, deep gulleys, allowing the uneroded areas among them to remain as the visible spikes. The pits themselves come as the limestone rock is dissolved by water and carbon dioxide (which is slightly acidic). And the carbon dioxide to do this is contributed by the bacteria as they grow.

But why is this phenomenon—sometimes called *phytokarst*—not seen near all limestone cave entrances? In most nontropical places, the Sun, which is the growth source for the cyanobacteria, moves dramatically across the sky, changing its angle. So the growth of living things such as cyanobacteria is not uniform in one direction. But here, near the equator, the Sun's path is more uniform, coming from the same direction long enough (and strong enough) for the bacteria to grow, for long stretches of time, toward the Sun's light—the cave entrance.

EARLY MULU EXPLORATION

When the Gunung Mulu National Park area was explored originally, the cavers' adventures were quite dramatic. In Blue Moonlight Bay Cave, near Good Luck Cave, early explorers once got trapped as the river suddenly filled the cave after a tropical downpour. They had to swim out holding their breaths. In several other caves, cavers got infections when rodent feces entered their skin and bloodstream through ordinary rock scrapes and cuts. (Now antibiotics are taken along on cave tours.) In the park's caves with streams running through them, cavers used to get "Mulu foot"—small holes in their feet from other infectious organisms. Now it is known that feet must be kept dry.

Additionally, exploring Tiger Cave, also in the area, took five straight days of cliff climbing just to reach its high entrance. In the days before cave walkways were built in the park, cavers also had to walk right over the creatures on the cave floor. These include crickets large enough to eat birds' eggs, giant centipedes, cockroaches, beetles, and six-foot-(2-m-) long cave racer snakes. Some of these cave inhabitants eat the large amount of bat feces (guano) also found on the floor. Cavers typically had guano fall down on them almost constantly, like white dandruff. And, in some of the caves, injured or sick bats which had fallen to the cave floor occasionally bit them too.

CAVES OF LANGKAWI AND CAVE MATERIALS

The Langkawi islands lie off the tip of "Peninsular Malaysia," also called West Malaysia (the country includes part of the peninsula that holds Thailand). In these 104 islands, all dense rain forest, about 25 caves have been discovered, so far. Many more surely exist.

Formed from limestone, granite, and marble about 500–600 million years ago, the cave openings lie at the top of almost-sheer cliffs, are concealed behind tangles of mangrove trees, are visible only at low tide, or are home at their entrances to bees in giant beehives—and some also house rather aggressive wild monkeys. The caves which have been discovered here often have spectacular views outside and boardwalks built inside—and Malaysia is developing these caves for ecotourism.

Beyond the major construction materials that make up the body of caves—the layers of limestone, sandstone, and shale—they are composed of smaller amounts of other minerals. Of the 175 different minerals existing in limestone caves, the vast majority by volume is calcite. After that come gypsum, ice, aragonite, goethite (an iron mineral), and birmessite (a manganese mineral). Caves with large numbers of bats have an additional mineral: carbonate-hydroxylapatite.

This latter mineral is made of bat excretions (guano). Guano is rich in phosphorous (which comes originally from the shells of the insects the bats eat so voraciously). The bats' urine is rich in nitrogen. Fresh guano, made of about 4 percent phosphorous and about 12 percent nitrogen, decomposes and combines with cave calcite to make the carbonate-hydroxylapatite.

In bat-popular caves, their droppings contribute to the natural production of more than 40 other minerals also.

MULU EXPLORATION NOW

Though scientists and expert amateur cavers visit Gunung Mulu National Park regularly now, less experienced visitors are also welcome. An elaborate resort has recently been built just outside the park, from which people are taken by wooden motorboat to a built walkway for a two-mile (3.2-km) jungle stroll, then to a concrete path that leads quite far into Deer Cave, near Good Luck Cave. Lang Cave can also be visited as can part of Clearwater Cave and part of the Cave of the Winds (which has lots of stalactites and stalagmites), also nearby. These are the only Mulu caves open to the public, but they come complete with either secure cement or wooden pathways and lighting inside. It has become quite popular also to simply stand near cave entrances close to park headquarters at dusk, to watch all the bats come out for their nocturnal hunt.

Other park visitors can choose simpler housing in a nearby town and an outfitter/guide who provides supplies for swimming and climbing in deeper parts of caves such as Turtle Cave. River crossings can be a bit dangerous in the afternoons since near-daily rain raises water levels, so a good boat and guide are important. Out in the rain forest, the guides can even take visitors on Headhunters' Trail. There, one can see a canal built, literally, by headhunters on their path through this area—as recently as about 100 years ago.

Deer Cave, mentioned above, may offer the most to see, including the largest cave passageway in the world that is not considered a "chamber." No deer are present anymore, but the cave got its name when deer came to drink water at the west entrance. Millions of bats—of 12 different species—fly out of Deer Cave every evening, leaving to feed on insects as far as 50 miles (80.5 km) away. (Inside, they generate about three tons of guano every day.) This makes the inside of the cave warm and damp, smelling of ammonia from the chemistry of the guano decay. But there are streams, a pool to swim across, jumping spiders, hairy earwigs (an insect), assassin bugs, huntsman spiders (the size of a human hand), scorpions—and more.

At the end of this adventure comes the other entrance of Deer Cave called the Garden of Eden, a mile-wide area where the cave roof collapsed long ago. A garden of rain forest has grown there.

MANY CAVES HERE

The Mulu area is riddled with other dramatic caves. Some 15 of them plunge deeper than 350 feet (106 m) below the surface. And eight of them are longer than 12,465 feet (3,800 m). The longest, gua Air Jernih (*gua* means cave in the language of a local tribe), extends for 169,290

GUNUNG BUDA NATIONAL PARK, OTHER LARGE CAVE CHAMBERS

Directly north of Gunung Mulu National Park, another major national park is also part of the Sarawak state of Malaysia. *Buda* means "white" in the language of Penan, one of the tribes native to Sarawak, and this mountain is made of limestone light in color.

Inside this national park are many caves, with about 37 miles (60 km) of their passageways mapped so far. One of them, the Green Cathedral–Turtle Cave system is already the second largest in Borneo, though most of it still remains unexplored (and unmapped). Another, the East and North Buda Cave, has the deepest pit (vertical drop) in all of Borneo.

Elsewhere in the world, nothing equals the Sarawak Chamber in surface area, but some chambers are close. The following is a list of the 10 largest cave chambers in the world, as measured by their surface area:

1. Sarawak Chamber (Malaysia)	1,751,288 square feet	(162,700 m²)
2. torca del Carlista (Spain)	824,731 square feet	(76,620 m²)
3. Majlis al Jinn (Oman)	624,307 square feet	(58,000 m²)
4. Belize chamber (Belize)	538,734 square feet	(50,050 m²)
5. salle de la Verna (France)	487,282 square feet	(45,270 m²)
6. gruta de Villa Garcia (Mexico)	439,383 square feet	(40,820 m²)
7. gruta de Palmito (Mexico)	427,650 square feet	(39,730 m²)
8. Kocain (Turkey)	400,417 square feet	(37,200 m²)
9. Carlsbad Cavern Big Room (United States)	357,469 square feet	(33,210 m²)
10. sótano de las Golondrinas (Mexico)	356,393 square feet	(33,110 m²)

feet (51,600 m). Many will surely prove even longer once connecting passageways are found.

FORMATION

The formation of the Gunung Mulu National Park caves began in earnest about 55 million years ago, though there was some folding of the land and mountain uplift during the *Cretaceous* too. The mountains in the center of the Borneo island began then to be seriously eroded by rivers, which deposited a deep layer of sand into the sea off Sarawak.

Underground layers needed for cave formation

By about 30–20 million years ago, this thick sand had compacted into sandstone, and, since the rivers had changed course (because the mountains and their drainage were in different places), not much more sand reached the sea at this stage. Clear ocean water lay above the sandstone layer. Corals and other tiny sea creatures lived in it in profusion. Their shelled bodies and other detritus gradually built up in a layer above the sandstone.

At about 10 million years ago, the corals and shells had compacted into their own layer, this one now limestone. Above it sluiced in a lot of mud (and some sand) from new rivers flowing down the mountains. The topography had changed because the whole island of Borneo was rotating in counterclockwise *plate tectonic* movements, and this crumpled the land. The mud and sand gradually compacted into shale, with thinner layers of sandstone in between.

After these periods of relative calm, *tectonic* processes in this area activated yet more strongly. By about 5 million years ago, the twisting of the land was causing the piled-up layers of sandstone, limestone, and shale to uplift and fold. Rock that had been underwater was lifted above the ocean surface too. Some geologists think that there were as many as seven different such processes. All this converging, colliding, and twisting created both minor and major cracks, *faults* in the uplifted masses.

These faults created excellent pathways for cave formation. The abundant tropical rainfall was easily able to carry water through them to below the surface. Surface soils, as usual, gave this water the slight acidity it needed to corrode the soft limestone rock. The rain also eroded the rock directly, especially the top layers, which were shale. This altered the shape of the mountains further. By the end of the period 5 million years ago, the mountains now in and near Mulu National Park were in the present location they occupy today (though, of course, their shapes continued to change through erosion and other forces).

Over the 5 million years that led up to today, more folding, faulting, and erosion has occurred. This is still a tectonically active area. Cave formation in limestone may be slow, but it has been very steady here. Since Sarawak lies so close to the equator, no snow falls to slow the water-dripping needed for cave building.

The caves seen here today probably all date back to between 3 and 1 million years old.

LOCAL GEOLOGY: OIL, NATURAL GAS, COAL, PEAT RESOURCES

Offshore of Sarawak, oil companies are already drilling deep into the sandstone layers of rock from the Middle to Lower *Miocene* period, about 20 to 10 million years ago. Now, onshore also, geologists are examining old, organic-rich sediments that appear coal-like, since they suspect that they could generate more oil. Oil and natural gas can form from coal which has been and is being compressed and heated far beneath the Earth's surface.

Coal itself can come from peat. Peat is a fuel (it can be drained and burned), but it also can be thought of as "loose coal." Both coal and peat come from organic-rich sediments that begin as rain forest leaf litter and other detritus. This material is piled up and compressed each year in low-oxygen conditions that do not allow much of it to decompress until it is thick and more or less uniform in composition. As this material becomes buried deeper and deeper under more and more layers of forest litter, it thickens further and forms what is known as peat. Sarawak's many rivers, river plains, and river deltas are rich in peat, accumulated mostly over the last 7,500 years. Whole leaves have even been found .6 mile (1 km) down, though this is unusual. The acidity of the peat preserved a few of them.

Geologists who research resources such as these are called economic geologists.

RAIN FOREST TREE RESOURCES

Biologists and ecologists in international teams also are studying the rain forest near Gunung Mulu. Rain forest covers a full two-thirds of Sarawak. In it, they have already inventoried some 2,500 different tree species, 5,500 flowering plants, and more than 20,000 animal and insect species, in an area only within about 30 miles (48 km) of the Sarawak Chamber. There are surely more to be found.

So far, two of the tree species seem to manufacture a substance that works against the HIV virus; one makes an anti-inflammatory medicine; and others produce rubber, cooking oil, and more. Though it may seem strange that trees "grow" medicines, it is not. Trees produce substances for their own purposes—usually to deter or poison invading insects—that, by coincidence, may match humans' needs. Many of the medicines now in the human pharmacopoeia came originally from plants. Their chemistry was then copied in our labs. Aspirin is only one example: It comes from the bark of one kind of willow tree. (Using nature as a model has become a trend in science. The book that best describes this is *Biomimicry*, in the bibliography.)

The potential resources of Sarawak's rain forest are at risk, however, since the rain forests themselves have been cut down considerably since the 1970s—by both the timber companies and the rural people.

RAIN FOREST WATER RESOURCES

Sarawak's rain forests are also valuable for the moisture "work" they do for the planet's atmosphere. Worldwide, tropical rain forests cover about 12 percent of the land surface, but they hold about 40 percent of the carbon. As this carbon "bank" shrinks with deforestation, previously stored carbon dioxide is released. This enhances the *greenhouse effect*, a gradual warming of the planet not particularly good for present life-forms, such as humans. Rain forests also evaporate, or transpire, a lot of water to the atmosphere, "exhaling" this moisture once received as rain. This engenders clouds and new rain, here and elsewhere.

Scientists have measured the "breath" of one large area of Sarawak's rain forest, partly to use it as a benchmark. The rain forests here are different from those in Amazonia since Sarawak experiences no real dry season. Dry spells do occur now and then, but not in a distinct pattern, and the rain, temperature, and sunlight do not vary much over a year. The forest's evaporation of water has been studied at different levels, from ground level up to the tree foliage canopy. A giant crane that stands 262 feet (80 m) tall, equipped with sensors and an elevator, has been used to collect data for scientists working on rain forest preservation.

If Sarawak's rain forests are allowed to remain largely in place, the water that does not evaporate but rather drips down through the acidic leaf litter and soils will be able to enlarge the caves, too, very gradually but steadily.

IN THE FIELD: DYE TRACES

A low-tech technique in cave studies, but a very useful one, is the dye trace. Cave explorers in Gunung Mulu National Park suspected that there were more connections among the caves—and more caves entirely—than were known, and they determined to find them.

In an area of the park called Hidden Valley, a stream vanishes down the slope of the Mulu mountain. Where does it go? Into what cave?

It took two dye traces to figure this out. Green dye was first added to the area where the stream was still visible. The cavers expected it to come out in an aboveground spring called Clearwater Spring. It did not.

But, continuing to force their way through the rain forest, they found green color in the Paku River a few miles away—though no cave. Earlier, however, they had noticed another spring pouring out of another cave into this same river, but in a different stretch of it. They put green dye in again (the first batch had flowed away quickly, as it always does) and watched the whole area.

The second batch of green water then indeed appeared in a cave, which they named Good Luck Cave. This is the cave that holds the Sarawak Chamber.

IN THE FIELD: MUD POLARITY

The Mulu caves are home to countless water pools, and most feature mud brought in when the local rivers flood. The mud layers on the bottom of the still pools are older than those on top. This mud can be used to help figure out the age of the cave, which will be older than the oldest mud, but not too much older since the flooding happens so regularly.

The way to date mud is to look for its magnetic orientation, its polarity. Some of the mud has iron-rich minerals in it, and those function as tiny magnets. Like a bar magnet in a physics lab, they have a north-south polarity. This is important because that polarity was set when the particle's original molten rock cooled, locking in that magnetic polarity, which matched the north-south polarity of the planet at that time. The Earth's magnetic poles have reversed themselves many times since our planet solidified—about every 250,000 years, on average—and the phenomenon is not well understood, though it seems to involve seething plumes moving down in the Earth's *mantle*. The known dates of polarity reversals are used as yardsticks.

The Sarawak Chamber and the cave that contains it are truly unusual. This is the largest such chamber found anywhere, in any natural cave, in the world.

5

Kazumura Cave of Hawaii

United States

Created by Kilauea, an active vent of the Mauna Loa volcano in Hawaii, this cave is a horizontal tube of hardened lava. It was built, expanded, and hollowed out over a period of about 50 years of volcanic eruptions. Kazumura (also spelled as Kazamura) is the longest lava cave in the world and one of the deepest. Among its features are about 82 different entrances, frozen lava waterfalls, dark-gray, glassy-looking walls, "windows," and some stalactites and stalagmites that look nothing like those in a limestone cave. Its age of 350–700 years old also makes it, like all lava caves, much younger than a typical limestone cave.

Lava caves, also called lava tubes, form in a way completely different from the way limestone caves do. There is no dripping water percolating through and dissolving limestone—the most common method of cave construction and characteristic of the caves in many other chapters of the book. No flowing water sculpts these caves either. Instead, formation begins as a volcano spews out thick rivers of *magma*. The outer layer of this molten lava, exposed to the air, hardens first, forming a rough aboveground "snake" shape. More of the lava sweeps along inside the hardening tube, like a river, forming downstream more of the "shell" or "rind" exterior. The tube extends farther and farther out from the volcano. When all the lava has finally flowed outward in that eruption, the tube is empty. The walls and roof harden further, and the cave is created. In a volcanic area such as Hawaii, this process happens often. Kilauea is probably the most active volcano in the world today—it has been erupting almost constantly since 1983, in its most recent phase of activity. It has made other lava caves, too, but none as long as Kazumura. Lava chambers, as opposed to full caves, are a separate but related phenomenon: A large gas bubble in the lava pops to form the hollow space.

It is the sheer size of Kazumura that is so amazing. This cave is more than 41 miles (65.5 km) long, as mapped so far, with the broadest passage at 69 feet (21 m) wide and 59 feet (18 m) high. Over part of its length—21 miles (34 km)—it moves downhill steadily, reaching a depth of 3,612 feet (1,101 m). This follows the slope of its "parent" volcano. The deepest single point plunges more than 3,600 feet (1,097 m) below its roof surface, making it the deepest lava cave in the United States.

Kazumura's shape is not as simple as the tube of a subway system, however, though sections of it resemble one. It is more like a crooked tree branch, laid on its side, with passages extending off like sticks from the main length, even some at upper levels. These features were created at different times during the years of eruption.

Located near Hawaiian Volcanoes National Park on the island of Hawaii (the largest of the Hawaiian islands, also called the "Big Island"), Kazumura is about 12 miles (20 km) south of the city of Hilo. Aboveground, the cave is covered with so much tropical vegetation that its presence is effectively concealed. Prehistoric Hawaiians did discover it, however, and used primarily its 5.5-mile (9-km) section nearest to the ocean. An image of Kilauea's lava can be seen in the lower color photo insert on page C-4.

LAVA CAVES BEYOND KAZUMURA

Hawaii has thousands of lava caves of all sizes. They form most readily when a volcano's eruptive magma is low in viscosity (not too thick), low or moderate in volume, and uniform in its flow. (This scenario is found often in Hawaiian volcanism.) Some of the caves are small enough for light to penetrate the whole tube, and these can be crawled though in a matter of seconds. Others, on the ocean floor, have been used as sites for scuba diving. Still others, such as Ainahou Ranch Cave, also proceeding from the Kilauea volcano, plunge almost as deep as Kazumura. Some are steep, buried in rain forest areas, and erode readily as flooding from the tropical rain flows through them and gradually dissolves the volcanic material. Some lava caves are even found inside the *caldera* of Kilauea and can be so high in temperature that special equipment (and nerve) is required to explore them. One unusual lava cave is crowded with pieces of lava crust. Most have ropey lava, called *pahoehoe*, as their floors. Hawaii is considered the most important place in the world to study lava caves since most of the lava erupted by its volcanoes moves through a tube of some size before cooling.

Wherever volcanism has produced lava flows, lava caves can exist. Those connected with Mount Etna in Italy have been studied extensively, as have the tubes on Réunion Island in the Indian Ocean, where one volcano has erupted about once a year for each of the last 50 years. Iceland also has many lava caves. The Craters of the Moon area of Idaho, parts of New Mexico, and areas of northeastern California have lava caves, too, as does Mount Saint Helens in Oregon.

Ancient, collapsed lava caves have also been discovered on the Moon, where they can easily be seen aboveground, like frozen snakes made of

In this image made by radar, the shape of the Kilauea volcano can be seen. *(NASA/ Visible Earth)*

rock, since there is no vegetation to obscure them. They also tend to be much bigger than Earth's versions and have even been discussed as housing for a future Moon base. It is possible that Mars has lava caves as well.

DIFFERENT FROM LIMESTONE CAVES

Though this type of cave does not typically compare in length or complexity to a limestone cave, the creation of a lava cave has an advantage: The process is so much quicker that it can be observed in action. Otherwise, they can be hard to find in Hawaii—at least until part of the roof collapses to expose an entrance into the hollow area beneath. Lava caves tend to be much younger than limestone caves simply because they do not last as long: Collapse continues and can easily overtake the entire structure.

For perspective on the different types of caves, please see the introductory chapter, "Origin of the Landform: Caves."

TINY LAVA TUBES

Only .00004 inch (1 to 9 micrometers) in diameter, the tiniest, most unusual, lava tubes are not created in an eruption. Even stranger, they seem to be the handiwork of microbes dissolving volcanic rock to use its chemical energy. Perhaps even more amazing, these tubes, found in

3.5-billion-year-old rock in South Africa, may be evidence of the earliest life on Earth. A microscopic creature would have had to burrow into the rock shortly after its formation to exist in rock this old. This research finding is still preliminary, with some scientists arguing that the tubes may be inorganic, not biological, and proceed from the chemistry of the volcanic rock as it hardens. Either way, this is a completely different, additional phenomenon from that which creates a lava tube such as Kazumura.

INSIDE KAZUMURA

The *speleothems* here bear no resemblence to those in a limestone cave such as Mammoth Cave or Carlsbad Caverns. They form in a different way. Here, as the inner surface of the cave roof cools, the lava degasses (gases in the volcanic magma evaporate) and also loses its water content. This allows thick drips and blobs to form, hanging down from the roof. They form out of iron oxide—rich vapors as the degassing causes the rocky walls to solidify. In Kazumura, a frozen "froth" decorates the ceiling in places, too, also a sign of degassing. Hawaiian volcanic gases contain lots of water vapor but also carbon dioxide, nitrogen, sulfur dioxide, and smaller amounts of other minerals such as the iron oxide.

These features form in a much shorter time than comparable features in a limestone cave, and their shapes are thicker and smaller. Some of them can be reddish or brownish, from the lavas at different stages of the volcano's eruption. Here in Kazumura, most are a dark gray.

The walls in this cave tend to be smooth, with ridges or blades that show the downstream direction the lava river took inside its hardening shell. Formations such as these usually result from an increase in lava speed in that specific area and sometimes even from wind acting on the molten lava. In other cave features, the upper passages, closer to the surface, tend to have uneven floors because of routine roof and wall breakdowns. Tree roots also have grown down into the cave.

The main cave passages are not always straight in Kazumura. This structure happens because lava flows take the route of least resistance, at any and every juncture. Less or more resistance can occur because the underlying rock may be weaker or stronger in one area. Roof breakdowns block the flow along certain paths, too, which can make for a crooked path. Passageways can even braid—split and then rejoin—as the lava flow breaks into smaller rivulets in places. In fact, Kazumura Cave probably formed as a braided system, some of the parts of which converged to make the main passageway. For more on flow issues, see "In the Field: Fluid Dynamics," at the end of this chapter. Erosion has also contributed to shaping the cave, especially thermal erosion here: Things can just melt.

CAVE FEATURE FORMATION

Though they may look a bit like the hollow pipes of a limestone cave's *stalactites*, the speleothems on the ceiling, floor, and walls of Kazumura are quite different. These stalactites develop during the cooling of a particular area, as lava partly crystallizes at temperatures of about 1,958 to 1,832°F (1,070 to 1,000°C). A typical Hawaiian lava flow begins at up to 2,150°F (1,175°C) at its source.

These cave features are typically much less than an inch (.7 cm) long but occasionally can exceed 3.25 feet (1 m). They are often not completely straight. Some look like, and are called, "lava roses," others like crooked worms. Still others look like barnacles, or little spatter cones, or toothpaste squeezes, or blisters. They are typically so rich in iron magnetite content that they could be picked up with a magnet.

MOST UNUSUAL FEATURES

Windows and waterfalls are also present in Kazumura—though all are made of rock that is solid now. The waterfalls can be up to 50 feet (15 m) high and usually form when flowing lava in an active lava tube erodes the floor and plunges into another, older tube area below (from a previous eruption). The second tube, stone cold, causes the waterfall to "freeze" in place. Some of Kazumura's waterfalls have "plunge pools" beneath them, also now solidified rock. More than 40 such waterfalls have been surveyed in Kazumura.

The cave windows, usually a few yards or so long (and not squared off) open during the flow of the lava. Some are shoved or punched out while the lava is warm, as the warm rock breaks down, and some form in an area of thinner crusts. Almost all of them become closed when plugged by more lava, but some do remain open inside the cave. Not a conduit or view to the outside, however, they are more like a gap in the wall.

LAVA UPON LAVA

The lava flows that made the Kazumura Cave flowed over yet-older lava from previous eruptions. (This is how the Hawaiian Islands formed out of the ocean to begin with, layer by layer, eruption by eruption.) Probably about six periods of eruption have left their layered evidence at this cave, three of them within the last 5,000 years. Flows have to be thick in one direction and be continuous over a long time, however, to create a cave, and this does not always happen.

LAVA CAVE DANGERS

Though few people would enter a lava cave while its originating volcano was erupting (even to do science), these caves present other dangers. Some of these hazards are a bit unusual, and dealing with them goes beyond the obvious rule not to walk on molten lava or to get near the real flames that occasionally are emitted by Kilauea in an eruption.

The first and most basic issue with lava caves is that the tube allows the lava flow to reach much greater distances from the volcano—farther and also much hotter than one might think. During one flow, the Kazumura Cave was found to lose only 39°F (4°C) in temperature over a length of 24 miles (39 km). Lava that stays that hot can flow for many miles, destroying property, before it solidifies, too. The lava tubes of Mauna Loa, the massive volcanic system of which Kilauea is a part, have directed molten lava across land and then down and along a slope of the seafloor as far as 1.9 miles (3.1 km) below the ocean's surface before chilling and solidifying. Kilauea itself fed lava to the sea through lava caves almost daily during the 1986–90 eruptive period and has done so many other times. Explosions of steam accompany the entrance of lava into the sea and can be exciting to see—from a distance.

The next hazard, which affects road, home, and other construction projects and their crews, is collapse. Hawaii has so many lava caves of all vintages, often concealed under vegetation, that equipment can crash right through the roof of an unknown cave onto the rock floor below. In Washington State, an accident in 2002 similar to this involved a canal—equipment broke through an undetected lava cave roof, damaged the bank of the canal, and thereby caused a flood. Even where the locations of the caves are fairly well known here, they may not have been completely mapped, creating some remaining accident potential. This risk does not disappear once a construction project ends. On one island in South Korea, engineers discovered that an existing road had been built to run right over a lava cave and created constant weight on its roof from all the traffic. It had held up, so far. They researched the stresses and decided that a tube three times as wide as its roof is thick could bear the burden of this particular road.

Road routes have been changed for other reasons besides danger of collapse. Some of the lava caves in Hawaii are also historic, scientific, and recreational/eco-sites and hence should not be disturbed.

Another issue is pollution. Some lava caves in Hawaii have been used as garbage dumps, hazardous waste disposal sites, even places for sewer pipe openings. Spring runoff can transport this material through the tubes, affecting groundwater drinking supplies faraway, as well as aboveground water quality downstream. Vandalism is another problem being addressed.

Though this is not common, some lava cave passageways hold deadly gases. This happens when the lava degasses as it cools but the gas is trapped in an area and not allowed to dissipate.

The image shows the entrance to the Thurston Lava Tube near Kazumura Cave.
(H. T. Stearns, U.S. Geological Survey)

OTHER LAVA CAVES

The Earth is a volcanic planet, and lava caves are not uncommon. Many are found in the highly volcanic country of Iceland. Kenya, Spain, and South Korea are also noted for theirs. And Thurston Lava Tube, in Hawaii Volcanoes National Park, not far from Kazumura, is itself a major site.

Thurston Lava Tube, also made by Kilauea, is actually the lava cave with the most visitors of any in the world. Its first 393 feet (120 m) have been lit electrically; its total length of about 1,460 feet (445 m) is easy walking since the walls and floor are smooth. Thurston lies in a rain forest, with tree ferns decorating its entrance.

(continues)

(continued)

Both Hawaii and Iceland are sites of the hotspot—style of volcanism, though Iceland also sits right on the boundary between two tectonic *plates* (the large North American and European plates), and Hawaii has no such plate boundary. The juncture of the plates here forms part of the much longer Mid-Atlantic Ridge. This is a major planetary landform that runs north and south down the middle of the Atlantic Ocean floor. From it, the Atlantic Ocean seafloor is expanding. Iceland is thus spreading out, too, from a broad "neovolcanic" zone that extends from north-central Iceland to the south, where it swings southwest. In chapter 10, on Kverkfjöll Cave of the Vatnajökull Glacier, this country's volcanism is further explored.

A major Icelandic lava cave, Three Peaks Cave, whose Icelandic name is Thrihnjukagigur, begins in the Blue Mountains only about 12 miles (20 km) from Reykjavík, the capital city. It is a vertical cave, opening from a mountain peak and descending about 656 feet (200 m) to its bottom. The shape is that of a wine bottle, the neck narrower than the base. One area of its wall, about 196 feet (60 m) down, features a kind of "balcony." Here, some Icelanders plan to create a viewing platform for ecotourists. Entrance would be via a new sloping passageway dug down nearby and built parallel to the cave, avoiding the vertical drop of the cave itself. This passageway would end at the new platform. Visitors could experience "dangling" in the cave without damaging it, the theory goes. Iceland also has numerous horizontal lava caves of all sizes, several of which are already open to visitors.

Around the world, lava caves do not typically reach the lengths or the depths as do the most impressive limestone caves. Nevertheless, some can be extensive. The deepest include

Leviathani Cave	(Kibwezi, Kenya)	1,339 feet	(408 m)
Ainahou Ranch Cave	(Hawaii, United States)	1,155 feet	(352 m)
cueva del Viento, Breveritas segment	(Canary Islands, Spain)	860 feet	(262 m)

The longest include

Majung-gul	(Je Ju Do, South Korea)	43,530 feet	(13,268 m)
Bilremos-gul	(Je Ju Do, South Korea)	38,547 feet	(11,749 m)
Kazumura Cave	(Hawaii, United States)	38,428 feet	(11,713 m)
Leviathani Cave	(Kibwezi, Kenya)	36,588 feet	(11,152 m)

CAVE ECOTOURISM

In Hawaii, several lava caves are open to the public. Two from elsewhere on the Mauna Loa volcano are very popular: Kaumana Cave and the Kulakai cave system. Laniakea Cave and Ka Eleku Cavern are Hawaiian visitor sites. Part of Kazumura can be walked, too, in a five-hour venture.

VOLCANIC CONNECTIONS?

Perhaps surprisingly, Hawaii's major volcanoes are not connected to each other in their lower "plumbing," the level of their *magma chambers.* (Ultimately, of course, all volcanoes connect to the same mantle of our planet.) Even though volcanoes have been erupting in this state for nearly 1 million years, each volcano has its own separate "stomach" of molten lava to draw upon. These chambers lie from 1.25 miles (2 km) up to 30 miles (48 km) deep under the surface.

KILAUEA ERUPTS

Kilauea, creator of Kazumura, is the most consistently active volcano under study since geology began as a science. A volcano observatory has been in operation right on the volcano for about 100 years. Kilauea's eruptions, often lasting for long periods of time, punch out slightly different varieties of lava, all of which have been monitored. One time, for four years on end, it emitted almost 10,595,000 cubic feet (300,000 m³) of lava every day. And, even when not erupting, Kilauea exhales carbon dioxide from its open vents. (This does contribute to the greenhouse effect, though in a natural way.)

The magma comes up into and flows from different vents on the body of the volcano, the flows usually 10–30 feet (3–9 m) broad, according to the history of the measurements. This volcano always seems to affect Hawaiians in some way, no matter what directions the flows take. Sometimes the molten rock ignites, burns, covers, and demolishes whole neighborhoods at once. Sometimes it cuts off homes by destroying the

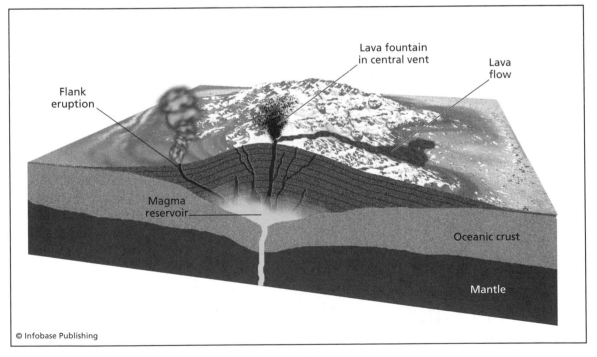

Shows the basic tectonic elements of a volcano such as Kilauea

road that leads to them. This can make for spectacular fireworks. New lava caves form often, while others are used by the volcano as its own private streets to the ocean. When flows pile up thick enough, whole new peninsulas of land can be added to the Hawaiian landmass.

Perhaps surprisingly, though, Kilauea is not particularly dangerous to people. This is because its flows, and those of all the Hawaiian volcanoes, are usually pahoehoe lava. This lava is slow and sluggish, like a fiery monster on the crawl, not the run. Because of the deep geology under Hawaii, which will be described later in the chapter, the lava here is very fluid. This means that the gases and other volatile elements in the lava can escape easily and gradually—rather than explosively. The lava, once cold, often becomes thick and ropey. Homeowners, pedestrians, and tourists can drive or walk out of the lava's way. One tourist did die here, however, in 1993, when the new lava he chose to stand on, at the edge of the ocean, collapsed into the sea. The slow flow is fortunate since this material is extremely hot—usually to about 1,292°F (700°C).

The other kind of lava that proceeds commonly from Hawaiian volcanoes such as Kilauea is called *aa*. It has a thick, brittle crust, making it sharp. As it tumbles along, it piles up and breaks off into skin-slicing boulders and smaller rocks. Though aa can create a lava cave—when the aa is covered with pahoehoe—this is unusual.

Hawaiian eruptions usually begin with some explosive activity, such as *lava fountains* shooting up from opening vents. This lava is highly fluid and cools to become showers of *tephra*. Tephra looks like black sand but is actually ash. In Hawaii, it is usually seen mainly near the vents. As tephra cools, some of it solidifies and consolidates further, making *tuff*. Once weathered, the tuff is no longer black but looks like tan cement, though it is actually lava.

Relatively little of this tuff material is visible in Hawaii because the eruptions settle down so quickly into pahoehoe and aa lava flows. And new eruptions are always emitting more lava to cover the old flows. Geologists can study the pahoehoe for its porosity, the tiny empty spaces where the gas bubbles popped during cooling. This helps them understand the nature of the eruption. Elsewhere in the world, where volcanic eruptions are more explosive, it is common for the final rock to be andesite and rhyolite, tan and speckled gray minerals, respectively. (The various rock types emitted in volcanic eruptions depend on both the chemistry of the underlying mantle and whether "recycled" crustal rock is mixed into it.)

LAVA COMPOSITION

The lava in Hawaii tends to be very black, made of basalt. This hardened magma is rich in iron and magnesium overall but is not as rich in iron as the lava in some other places. The iron content looks reddish in the cold lava.

The basalt here also looks a bit glassy since it is composed of myriad microscopic crystals. The crystals themselves are a calcium-rich feldspar mineral called plagioclase. Also in the basalt is the mineral pyroxene (made mostly of silica, iron, and magnesium), the mineral olivine, and iron pyrites.

This basalt is a deep-Earth material, flowing up from the crust and even from the mantle of the Earth below. Vast stirrings of molten rock called *mantle plumes* seem to be the energy behind the eruptions that make volcanoes and their lava caves like Kazumura. They originate far down within the Earth.

Basalt is not a rare material—it is the most common rock on Earth. Most, if not all, of the black rock that can be seen around yards, parks, or anywhere, is basalt. The ocean floors are made of it and so, long ago, was the land, though it has been covered up now with soils and other material in most places. Weathered basalt is often gray or reddish.

But the eruptions in Hawaii emit very new, fresh, and therefore black basalt. It comes up from the crust and mantle about 62 miles (100 km) down. In the currently most widely accepted theory, the eruptions are common underneath Hawaii because this area lies where a mantle plume meets the crust. The phenomenon is called a *hot spot*. A hot spot can remain in one place for millions of years. It is as though the planet is panting—and the heat keeps coming up here. The source of this heat is the decay of radioactive materials in the core of the Earth.

HAWAIIAN ISLAND ARC

Looking at Hawaii's islands is like looking at the footprints of the hot spot. But, contrary to appearances, it is not the hot spot that has moved. Instead, it is the Hawaiian islands themselves, through the process of

In this aerial, the Hawaiian Islands' path looks like footsteps across the Pacific. (*NASA/Visible Earth*)

plate tectonics. Riding on the crust, they have moved over the buried hot spot, forming one by one.

Hawaii sits near the middle of the Pacific plate, which slowly moves along, taking Hawaii with it. This plate is one of the seven major tectonic plates that, along with the eight medium and about 20 smaller plates, push against, over, under, and alongside each other, like pieces of a giant jigsaw puzzle with wheels under every piece.

The Earth's plate movements vary in speed, though all move more slowly than hair grows. It is just that they have been shoving along for nearly 3 billion years, time enough to open and close whole oceans. This has allowed land plenty of time to pass over a hot spot.

As the Pacific plate moved over the hot spot here, the upwelling lava emitted by the resulting hot spot volcanoes formed one Hawaiian island after another, creating the archipelago form seen on a map. The oldest island is Kauai in the northwest of the island arc, followed by Maui, Oahu, Molokai, and Lanai, in order, up to Hawaii, or the Big Island. The latter is the youngest and in the southeast section of the island arc. One by one, seafloor volcanism has punched up these islands. Kauai is about 5 to 7 million years old. The volcanoes on the Big Island, including Kilauea, are as new as today. This island is still forming.

None of the Hawaiian Islands was born instantly. Because of the ocean's immense depth, it can take many long and massive eruptions to build up an island (not until it breaks the surface of the sea does it gain the name "island"). The Mauna Loa and Mauna Kea volcanoes are, when their bases on the ocean floor are included, more than 30,000 feet (9,000 m) high. Since they continue to erupt, this means the Big Island is still swelling higher, as well as extending its reach into the sea in places.

Readers might want to watch the sea about 20 miles (30 km) southeast of the Big Island. Here the newest Hawaiian island will be emerging from the sea—in about 50,000–100,000 years. Geologists are observing it as successive undersea eruptions build up its "land." It has been growing for about 100,000 years already and has risen about 15,000 feet (4,500 m) off the ocean floor. In 1996, however, an immense eruption collapsed part of its summit, shrinking instead of building the height of the structure. This hidden event scattered rock over a six-mile (10-km) area. More eruptions will surely build the mass back up. This "island" already has been given a name, Loihi.

IN THE FIELD: VARIETY OF TECHNIQUES

Lava caves are studied by geologists in many ways. Some projects use high-resolution radiometers (heat meters) from airplanes to scan the lava as it flows. Once an eruption calms, other researchers direct *seismic waves* and other powerful waves into the lava. These techniques can locate lava caves since the waves are absorbed by open spaces rather than being transmitted through solid rock. They can also reveal areas that are especially porous even if no cave exists. Magnetic surveys are also used to gauge cave locations and discern the geochemistry of the lava, since lavas that are richer in iron are more strongly magnetic. Ground-penetrating radar, a relatively new technique, is also employed to map the hidden structure of the lava flows.

Once scientists and other explorers can get into the caves easily, they use basic equipment from compasses to fiberglass tape in mapping the cave. Connections among caves can be especially difficult to discover since even a very narrow rock barrier can make another passageway completely undiscernable.

Whether Kilauea is erupting or not, its slope is conveying a great deal of information to *volcanologists*. This volcano is "decorated" at all times with at least 60 *seismometers*, for example. These detect the often tiny earthquake volleys that can mean an eruption is imminent. *Tiltmeters* are also used to detect the very small new tilts or bulges on the volcano as the land stirs and swells; this happens as supplies of molten lava are building up below. Changes in the gases emitted at the vents and in the shapes of monitoring holes dug in the old lava are also watched. All this equipment is set up to transmit data automatically to the lab. The geologists often need to remain there for safety.

IN THE FIELD: FLUID DYNAMICS

The flow of lava, just as the flow of water and other materials, is the subject for researchers in fluid dynamics and, related to it, heat dynamics. This kind of study crosses many fields, is quite complex, and is used at Kilauea by geologists.

To picture fluid dynamics, think about a wide river upstream and a narrow canal downstream from it. Release a large amount of water into the upstream river, watch it flow, then also watch its flow as it enters the narrow canal. Where does the water flow the fastest? It is in the narrow canal, which must move the same water volume as in the wider area of the flow. In the narrower canal, the water will be more turbulent, too, swirling into many eddies as it barrels its way along.

Both a canal like this and a lava cave are both types of "Venturi tubes," and the relationship of flow diameter and speed is called the Bernoulli effect. The situation is similar in the cavities of jet engines, where gas is the flowing material. A lava cave is an interesting variant. First, the lava begins extremely hot, flowing faster and with more turbulence. Then it loses heat as it flows. Some of that heat is absorbed by the cave's walls and floor (though the lava stream moves too fast to actually melt them).

As the lava loses more heat, it loses some velocity and becomes a different type of fluid with, generally, lower turbulence. If scientists know the viscosity (thickness) of the lava, the slope of the tube, and the strength of gravity, they can use equations known from fluid dynamics to estimate the velocity of the lava and its gradual loss of heat. With this information in hand, they are next able to measure the heat at the Earth's surface—over the lava tube—to learn about the depth, size, and temperature of the buried cave during an eruption.

Fluid dynamics/heat dynamic studies are also used to study the degassing of the lava. As it cools, its gases escape (very gradually), and the heat loss can be measured. This research also leads to information on the ways lava caves meander (as rivers do) and even braid (from different channels/passageways that recombine). Conditions in the rock before the cave formed also direct the flow of the lava river. Scientists who engage in this kind of study are known as geophysicists or volcanologists.

Fingal's Cave of Scotland

Great Britain

Off the west coast of Scotland, seven miles (11.25 km) west of the Island of Mull and six miles (9.65 km) north of the Island of Iona, lies the small island of Staffa. It is just a quarter-mile (.4-km) wide and three-quarters of a mile (1.2 km) long. Part of it can be seen in the color insert on page C-5. On its southern tip, open to the force of the North Atlantic Sea, is Fingal's Cave. This is a cave so unusually beautiful that the composer Felix Mendelssohn wrote music in honor of it and the poet William Wordsworth composed poetry about it. It is also a geological marvel.

Fingal's Cave is the only sea cave in the world made entirely of hexagonally jointed *basalt*, also known as columnar basalt. The rocks form columns, making an archway 20–40 feet (6–12 m) high and rising to 300 feet (91 m) high in places. The vertical columns look like a harp frozen in stone or the pipes of a gigantic church organ, now silent. Where the

The entrance to Fingal's Cave is framed in columns of basalt. *(National Trust for Scotland)*

rock columns have split, the horizontal surfaces form a carpet mosaic of stepping stones, each a foot or two (.5 m) in diameter. Arcing over the cave's roof lies green turf dotted with sea birds, along with a few sheep brought over to graze in summertime. The whole of Staffa Island is a park belonging to the National Trust of Scotland.

Fingal's Cave is not large—only 227 feet (69 m) deep, just 70 feet (21 m) high from the water level to the roof, open to the sea on both ends, and with no particular *speleothems*. It is ornate because of the basalt columns, formed when fiery lava met cold sea about 60 million years ago. Some of the molten rock was instantly quenched, and evidence of this can be seen in the cave's ceiling. Other areas cooled more slowly, contracting and cracking to form the columns. Since then, the relentless power of the North Atlantic waves has been carving the cave from this solid rock, as can be seen in the color insert on page C-5.

Sea caves are not, in general, rare. As will be described later in the chapter, oceans have been opening and closing on the planet for 2 or 3 bil-

---

STAFFA ISLAND

Staffa Island features some caves smaller than Fingal's, excellent wildlife viewing, and interesting history. It can be visited by ferries leaving from several different nearby Scottish ports, though no accommodation or camping is available or allowed on the island.

Of the six caves that can be seen on the map on page 71, Clamshell Cave, Boat Cave, MacKinnon's Cave, and Cormorants' Cave are the main ones. All are sea caves, as is Fingal's, and all are best seen from the sea.

Clamshell Cave, which is a short walk from Fingal's, has some columnar basalt that has bent and curved away from the ocean. Boat Cave and MacKinnon's Cave are hollowed out of the *tuff* layer of ancient lava, the lava hardened into a cement-like rock below the basalt layer. Though it lacks the basalt columns, Boat has yellow walls sculpted by the sea and MacKinnon's has the most sea birds. Cormorants' Cave has a narrow opening and a tunnel that reaches MacKinnon's. This path can be walked at low tide on a calm day.

The wildlife here is typical of North Atlantic sites. Land birds include larks, wheatears, rock pipits, and starlings. Seabirds such as puffins, cormorants, shags, fulmars, black-backed gulls, razorbills, oyster catchers, terns, and kittiwakes abound, as do sea creatures from seals to salmon, lobsters to mackerel. Whale watching by boat is a popular activity here also.

Popular now, Staffa was even a faddish destination in Victorian times. About 300 visitors a day traveled here then, including Queen Victoria herself. In those days, the island had a few full-time inhabitants. They lived in cottages made from broken basalt columns and raised sheep.

Staffa has had eight different owners since its exploration in 1772 by Sir Joseph Banks, which brought it to national attention in Britain and, ultimately, to its status as public land. He was a noted scientist and explorer on his way to investigate Iceland. Banks wrote that the island is "one of the greatest natural curiosities in the world . . . the Giant's Causeway in Ireland . . . (is) but a trifle(s) when compared to this island," as quoted in the book *The Island of Staffa* (see bibliography).

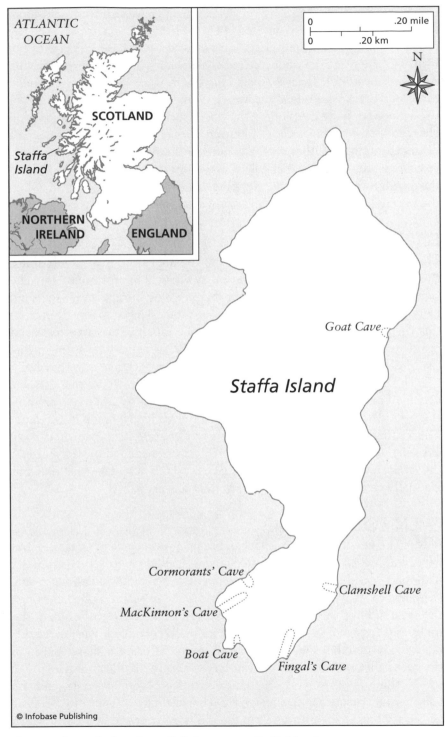

The map shows the locations of all the caves on Staffa Island.

lion years. For more than 2 billion years, glaciers have also come and gone, causing sea levels to rise and fall. (The *Pleistocene*, occurring over the past 2 million years, is only glaciation's most recent phase.) Sea caves can form anywhere waves pound at rock (especially rock easily dissolvable, such as limestone). Even seasonal changes in water levels can gradually carve out caves where land meets sea. Some sea caves later become entirely flooded, lying deep under the ocean surface. (As was mentioned in chapter 4, on Kazumura Cave of Hawaii, these can become sites for scuba divers to explore.) Other caves can become stranded on land, where they lose the name "sea cave." Fingal's Cave is intermediate. It can be walked through, on top of the basalt "stepping stones" that edge the water, when the ocean is calm, but it becomes "drowned" when the sea is rough.

FORMATION

The island of Staffa and other islands in the area are the lands left above the water level after a thick blanket of lava flowed in profusion here. The lava flooded in when the landmasses that are now Europe and Greenland were pulling apart and the continental *crust* split. *Magma* poured out from this deep fissure and hardened to make the basalt. This large-scale and more or less violent (depending upon time and place) process is the engine that created ocean floor all over the planet, from ancient times to today.

The massive continental split here was the birth of the Atlantic Ocean. This ocean was not yet in existence 60 to 53 million years ago, the period when lava began to flow into the widening crack in the land. This rifting apart (and joining together) of continents is known as *plate tectonics*. The "crack" here in the Earth's crust widened until it became the Atlantic Ocean seen today, with Staffa Island in it. The rock that was gradually carved into Fingal's Cave is thus this ancient.

EVEN LONGER AGO

Before the era of the Atlantic Ocean began, a more ancient ocean existed here, wider even than the Atlantic is today. Called Iapetus, it was a major planetary feature during the *Ordovician* of 505 to 438 million years ago. Evidence of its western shoreline, now spread very faraway but once just the west side of the crack in the crust, can be seen by geologists in the rocks and fossils of Newfoundland. It can also be traced, with more difficulty, considerably south of here in Europe. Its eastern shore is seen in the rocks that are now part of Scandinavia and the Baltic countries.

Nothing is forever on a tectonically active planet like ours, and the continental crust began to squeeze together again here. The "bite" in Britain's coastline at the Solway Firth (an old fjord near the Scottish-English border) is an area where plates once joined together in an ancient land, a supercontinent called Rodinia. Its formation eliminated the Iapetus ocean entirely. Some leftover pieces of the old Iapetus ocean floor have been found near the Welsh-English border.

Readers may have heard of the supercontinents Pangea and Gondwana. They are infants compared to Rodinia. Pangea was the Earth's dominant land feature from the end of the Paleozoic era through the Triassic and into the Jurassic (from about 270 million to about 150 million years ago). Gondwana was the name for the major continental grouping even longer ago, from about 500 to 400 million years ago. Rodinia was the major land-mass yet before that, about 1 billion years ago, in the late *Precambrian*.

Geologists, as rock sleuths, are now at work finding evidence pointing to an even older supercontinent, one whose heyday was about 1.5 billion years ago. There is little left of it. So far, it does not even have a name. Geologists of the future may be the ones to find the evidence and to name it.

LAVA LAYERS LEFT

Formations such as those at Fingal's Cave are built in layers. A major tectonic event causes the lava to flow for a few months or years at a time, usually with shorter breaks in between these eruptive periods. The deep base of Staffa Island, once above water, is ash and cinders compacted into a hard rock called tuff. The lava flow that formed it here originally (and in all the islands of the area) was 16–98 feet (5–30 m) thick and of the *pahoehoe* type also seen commonly in Hawaii and Iceland.

The cave's famous basalt columns lie above the tuff layer and probably formed in their own single eruption event. Above the columns, the highest rock layer is composed of broken-up basalt columns and other volcanic debris. Some of these are swirled and twisted, but in other places, one can walk on top of flat, broken columns similar to those at the cave floor level. At the entrance to the cave, the low columns are decked in green seaweed and yellow lichen. On top of all these rock layers lie soil and grass. The island is a little like a lava club sandwich with lettuce on top.

The whole island of Staffa, except for the part to the east of Fingal's, tilts about 4° down from west to east. As the Atlantic Ocean was forming, the rock mass that made Staffa was near enough to the actual fissure to lie at that angle. This tilting stressed the rock, cracking it. That made it easier for the cave to form later.

Glaciers also blanketed the land, eroded the island, and scraped off the top layers. For a chart of the period of glaciation, see chapter 10, Kverkfjoll Cave and the Vatnajökull Glacier, Iceland.

IN THE FIELD: GIANT'S CAUSEWAY

Giant's causeway, not too far from Fingal's Cave, though on Ireland's north coast, has the same dramatic columnar basalt, formed at about the same time and in the same way as Fingal's. Both are part of the same flood basalt or outpouring of lava that launched the Atlantic Ocean. The Giant's Causeway has received more research attention, however, since it is larger and more accessible. Its name comes from its own large, flat stepping stones of column tops that look as though only a giant could have made them—and for other giants to use as steps.

Seven different lava flows have been investigated here, within two main layers. Thin bands of soil lie in between, where the lava weathered between eruptive floods. The appearance is lasagna-like; each layer of hot lava pushed up onto the older one as the brand-new Atlantic Ocean was in its first stages of tectonic opening. Geomorphologists also note steep cliff areas where the lava mass simply cracked off in a phenomenon called shear force failure. This is happening here still and can present a danger to visitors walking the lower paths after heavy rainfalls.

How the columns form is a primary research issue, and this has been studied in a variety of ways. Focusing on the way random cracks become more regularly involved, in one study, drying a mixture of laundry starch and water. The evaporation of the water served as a substitute for heat loss in the lava. Another team of researchers analyzed the chemistry of the last stages of the lava as it cooled, and still others the way the cracks developed. Because temperatures can differ slightly on the surface of the cooling lava, hexagonal cracks appear and gradually penetrate deeper into the solid rock, following the path of least resistance.

Fingal's Cave is an unusually decorative lava cave. It was formed as a volcanic eruption met the sea, resulting in elaborate basalt columns.

Waitomo Cave of New Zealand

7

Waitomo Cave is a limestone cave lying in the northwestern part of New Zealand's North Island, one of the country's two major landmasses. (The other is the South Island.) Nearby is the highly *tectonic* Lake Taupo region, and the whole country is part of the Pacific *Ring of Fire*, shuddering and sparking regularly with earthquakes and volcanoes. With its 28 miles (45 km) of passageways, Waitomo is the largest and most elaborate glow-worm cave in New Zealand, if not the world. This unusual feature will be described later in the chapter.

The tectonic activity in New Zealand proceeds from its position vis-à-vis two of the major *plates* of the planet. The Indo-Australian plate, on which most of the North Island sits, is pushing past and partly over the Pacific plate, on which most of the South Island lies. The result, called *slip faulting*, is a characteristic of the Ring of Fire. Though the South Island has even more Earth action than the North, the North Island is geologically younger and its Taupo Volcanic Zone produces not only eruptions but also lots of hot springs; here, near Waitomo Cave, the groundwater percolates up through rocks heated by belowground tectonic activity and arrives warm at the surface.

The grinding, shoving, and separating of the tectonic plates in New Zealand has been going on for a long time. The country's landmasses separated from Antarctica and Australia about 80 million years ago. Lots of additional geologic instability occurred during the *Cenozoic*, especially in the Late *Oligocene* period of about 30 million years ago. Both tectonic activity and glaciation continued to come and go, and, by about 5 million years ago, New Zealand had finally been uplifted enough to take on its present shape.

The Oligocene left plenty of limestone here, and Waitomo Cave lies in a formation of it about 328 feet (100 m) thick. This kind of rock is built from the compacted bodies of ancient sea creatures, which indicates that the Waitomo land area was once on the ocean floor. About 4 million years were required to lay down the limestone material there. A local period of tectonic uplift occurred here about 12 million years ago, raising this area above the ocean surface. This set the stage for the hollowing out of Waitomo Cave.

KARST TERRAIN

Once raised above sea level, the limestone of the Waitomo area was open to the subtropical rainfalls sweeping over the island. All this rain, dripping down through the vegetation and then the porous limestone rock, gradually carved out Waitomo and other caves in the area. (For more on how limestone caves form, see chapter 1, on Mammoth Cave of Kentucky, in the United States.) The process also gradually created the *speleothems* such as stalactites and stalagmites found in the cave. Some of these formations at Waitomo can be seen in the upper color insert on page C-6.

Near Waitomo Cave are *sinkholes*, dry valleys, disappearing rivers, and natural arches and bridges where other caves have collapsed. So geologists believe many more caves remain to be discovered in this area of karst terrain.

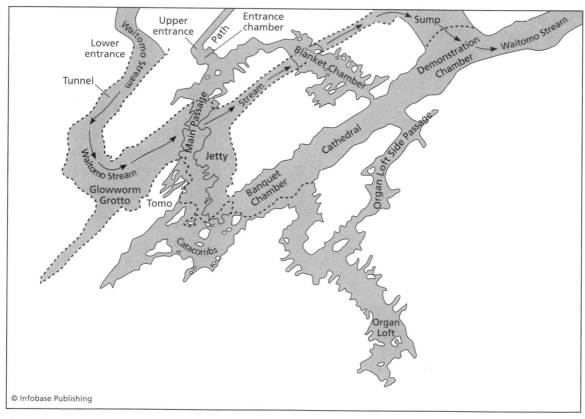

Shows the shape and major chambers of Waitomo Cave

ANCIENT CLIMATE

Geologists can use the speleothems inside caves to learn more about climate history, and studies such as these have been performed in neighboring caves within Waitomo's karst terrain. The key is to analyze the *isotopes* or variants of the oxygen in the water that was locked into the cave formations as they formed, drip by drip, over hundreds or thousands of years.

The way it works is as follows: Water from various sources is not uniform at the molecular level. Evaporated ocean water, coming down as rainfall in a significant dry period such as one where glaciation is widespread, is a little different chemically from water that has swirled in vast thunderclouds during a long, wet period. So the speleothems of Waitomo Cave can be used as a key to climate about 10,000 years back, a bit like dating a tree by the rings in the trunk.

This high-ceiling chamber inside Waitomo Cave shows some of the glowworms on the limestone rock wall and ceiling.   *(Brian Brake/Photo Researchers, Inc.)*

NEW ZEALAND CAVES

As an island nation in the vast Pacific, New Zealand has a great deal of karst terrain, its limestone formed from the fossilized bodies of sea creatures, as was mentioned. Because of uplift from plate tectonic processes, many of the caves are now well inland. And most are home to glowworms, firefly-like insects that do not fly. Instead, they glow and, in vast numbers, present an impressive sight.

Most of New Zealand's caves occur in two main areas. The first area rich in caves is the Waitomo region one on the North Island, named the same as the cave. None of the caves here are on the list of New Zealand's 20 deepest. But nine of them are among the country's longest caves. These include Gardners Gut Cave, the Mangawhitikan Cave System, Fred Cave, Thunderer Cave, Kuratani Cave, Ruakiri Cave, Waipura Cave, Kairimu Cave, and Cloaca Maxima. They range from 39,009 feet (11,890 m) to 11,155 feet (3,400 m) long. And they tend to have many speleothems in their upper passageways.

New Zealand's other cave region is on the South Island, in the Nelson region. Here, some of the caves are found in Oligocene limestone of about 40 million years ago (as is the case in Waitomo), but others have burrowed down deeper, into Ordovician marble that formed about 500 million years ago. Most of these caves have not been explored.

The record-holder for cave depth and a cave noted for its significant travel-through experience (with no need to retrace one's steps) is Nettlebed Cave. It extends 2,916 feet (889 m) down. Not discovered until 1969, its full depth and length were established in stages between then and the mid-1980s. Other extremely deep caves in this South Island region are Bulmer Cavern, H. H. Hole, Greenlink Cave, Windrift Cave, Harwood Hole–Starlight Cave, Gorgoroth Cave, Gormenghast, Blackbird Hole, Laghu Hole, and many others. These range from 2,388 feet (728 m) to 1,007 feet (307 m) deep.

One cave, Aurora Cave in the town of Te Anau on the South Island, is the 17th-deepest and the sixth-longest cave in the country, though it is not in either of the two main cave regions of the country. This is a spectacular place to visit—especially to view the glowworms on a tour of the section called the Te Anau Glowworm Cave. Both the Aurora and Te Anau Caves are part of the large Aurora–Te Anau Cave System.

Deep down in limestone thought to be about 35 million years old here, both surface water seepage and the flow of the Tunnel Burn River have been hollowing out this Te Anau Cave for at least 230,000 years in the upper part of the cave to about 15,000 years ago in the lower part. Rainfall is heavy in the area, and this cave is still forming today.

Inside, the roar of the water is as loud as the glowworms are silent. As one's eyes adjust to the darkness, while sitting still in a boat, the glowworms appear everywhere, as though thrown onto the ceiling and walls like tiny, glowing diamonds. They do not move (or drop down onto visitors).

Glowworms are the pupal stage of a type of fly called the fungus gnat. (The first two stages are as an egg, then larva, and the glowworm becomes a true fly for just a few days at the end of its life.) The glowworm stage attaches itself to the rock of the cave; spins out tiny, short threads like fishing lines; and hopes that small insects, such as mosquitoes brought inside by the river, will come to it. The light is the way it attracts the insects.

This strange system works well. Once a glowworm snares a dinner, it hauls the insect up to eat via its fishing line. The hungrier a glowworm is, the brighter it glows. After catching prey, it dims a bit for awhile. But in Te Anau Cave, as in the other glowworm caves of New Zealand, thousands upon thousands of the glowworms are bright enough to see all at once, day or night. Waitomo, for example, has hundreds of thousands of glowworms.

These creatures also live outside of caves in New Zealand, often in grassy banks along rivers or pathways of any kind. Hence, the species is known as a *troglophile,* meaning that it loves caves but can also live outside this habitat.

In Mammoth Cave, a stalactite has grown down to meet a stalagmite growing from the floor up. *(National Park Service)*

Ceiling stalactites are numerous here, slender against a massive stalagmite. *(National Park Service)*

This aerial image from the National Aeronautics and Space Administration shows the Yucatán Peninsula of Mexico, home to many cenotes. *(NASA/Visible Earth)*

It is easier to find a cenote from an airplane than by walking through the jungle. *(Alexis Rosenfeld/SPL/Photo Researchers, Inc.)*

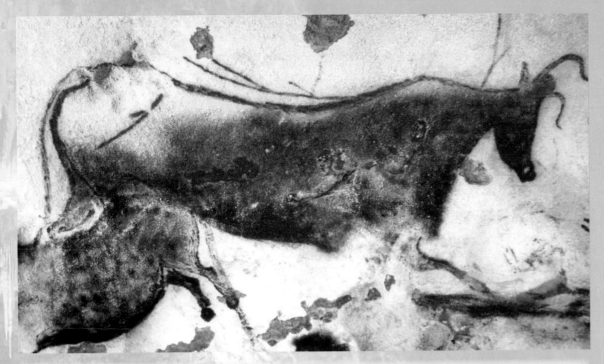

This photograph shows one of the animal paintings inside Lascaux Cave. *(Archivo Iconografico, S.A./Corbis)*

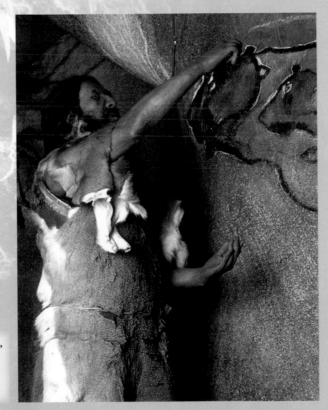

In this re-creation of a scene inside Lascaux Cave, a Cro-Magnon man paints an animal. *(Volker Steger/Nordstar-4 Million Years of Man/Photo Researchers, Inc.)*

The massive scale of Sarawak Chamber can be glimpsed in this image, which shows part of the chamber. *(Jerry Wooldridge, photographer)*

Kilauea's lava swirls from fiery red to black as it cools. *(Nasa/Visible Earth)*

Staffa Island, off Scotland, is home to Fingal's Cave. *(National Trust for Scotland)*

Entering Fingal's Cave at low tide when the sea is calm can be done using these natural stepping stones. *(National Trust for Scotland)*

The image shows flowstone, a speleothem in Waitomo Cave. *(Michael S. Yamashita, Corbis)*

The entrance to the Big Room of Carlsbad Caverns hints at its size. *(Harold W. Hoffman/Photo Researchers, Inc.)*

A tourist gazes at some of the stalactites and stalagmites of Carlsbad Cavern. *(Bruce Roberts/Photo Researchers, Inc.)*

Visitors and a ranger admire the box work speleothem in Wind Cave. *(National Park Service)*

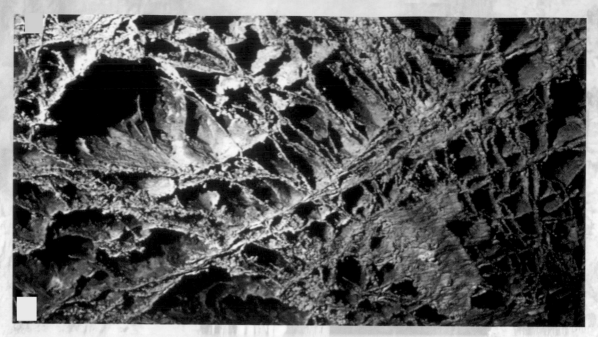

Ceiling box work is a distinct feature of Wind Cave. *(National Park Service)*

This interior view of the Kverkfjöll glacier cave shows the variety of ice and water inside. *(Ragnar Th. Sigurdsson, photographer)*

Results in the Waitomo area show that warmer and cooler periods have not been extreme over the last 3,900 years and that the coldest period here occurred about 3,000–2,000 years ago. Over the last 10,000 years, though, there have been naturally occurring variations of temperature of about 36°F (2°C) even in periods of just 100 years.

VISITING WAITOMO CAVE

The name "Waitomo" means "water entering a hole in the ground" in the indigenous Maori language. This reveals one way that limestone caves are often discovered. In 1887, a British surveyor and a local Maori chief explored a river entrance to Waitomo. About two years afterward, the cave began to be mapped and opened to the public.

Now it is possible for visitors to walk part of Waitomo Cave and boat through another section, seeing both the speleothems and the glowworms. More adventurous cavers can "abseil" or rappel down a 88-foot (27-m) cliff, go blackwater rafting or tubing, or even jet boating on the aboveground river. Nearby Aranui Cave can also be visited in an ordinary stroll.

ENVIRONMENTAL ISSUES

New Zealand geologists monitor Waitomo Cave (and other caves that receive visitors) for several key environmental factors. Among these are heat, carbon dioxide, water quality, human residues, and dust.

WHAT ELSE LIVES INSIDE NEW ZEALAND CAVES

New species are still being found in the caves of this country. Though these species are not yet well surveyed, scientists do know that, unlike the caves in many other countries, few bats or birds inhabit caves here. Rats, possums, frogs, eels, and an insect called the weta enter them but do not live their whole lives there. Hence they are known as *trogloxenes*.

Most of the true cave inhabitants—those that live their whole lives inside, the troglobites—are invertebrates (small creatures who lack backbones). Some are endangered species, since their habitat is so narrow. And more surveying of them is being done.

Scientists and other cavers use tiny traps to inventory these cave dwellers. These include "pitfalls," set up so that the insect tumbles into one while seeking the bait. Moldy cheese squares are also used, as are little rock "houses" with a flat rock held up by pebbles. The researchers also shine lights, since, though most cave species are blind, they do tend to be sensitive to light. Places searched in insect surveys are muddy ledges, tiny cracks in the wall, under stones, near streams, on damp walls where water is seeping down, and even inside the twigs lying on the cave floor and in the roots hanging down through the cave ceiling. Most cave creatures require high humidity, calm air movement, and avoid the areas that flood.

New Zealand's caves, scientists have found, are home to many species of beetle, tiny insects such as springtails, spiders, and millipedes. In or near steady water sources are small crustaceans such as the pseudoscorpion and cave cricket. More will surely be discovered by cavers of the future.

Fossilized birds extinct since the Ice Age, such as the brown teal, have also left their bones in New Zealand caves. These are wetland and forest birds that became trapped inside long ago.

Heat and carbon dioxide levels in Waitomo are highly correlated to the number of visitors. One person emits as much heat as a lightbulb of 82–116 watts. Tour groups also require electric lightbulbs, adding to the effect. Carbon dioxide is also exhaled by each visitor. Since carbon dioxide levels above 2,400 ppm can damage the speleothems, the number of visitors is monitored each day. Above 5,000 ppm, the carbon dioxide would also affect the visitors themselves; it is not what humans prefer to breathe.

Water quality inside Waitomo relates to the air's quality. After a major rainfall, water can enter the cave so fast that the trace pollutants in it—especially solvents and pesticides—do not have time to evaporate. In certain areas of the cave, notably the "Organ Loft," air circulation and ventilation are minimal. Only 90 people per hour are allowed to enter this area, and only in morning and late afternoon. Between 10:30 A.M. and 3 P.M. each day, this area of Waitomo Cave is usually closed entirely.

People also shed bits of hair, skin, and clothing, and often smoke particles and pollen are brought in too. Measurements have shown that one person releases one microgram (1/1000th of a gram) of "stuff" every second. If 1 million visitors spend one hour apiece inside a cave, by the end of 10 years, there are about 79 pounds (36 kg) of human residues in a cave. And these numbers include only the finest, airborne material. This material can boost algae and moss levels in a cave as well as erode the speleothems. And it is very hard to remove. Cleaning is sometimes done by spraying mist on the walkways.

Dust, the name used for the larger and also the tinier particles, can damage the aesthetics of one's experience in a cave. Cave officials in New Zealand sometimes conduct steam cleaning of an entire cave.

IN THE FIELD:
CONDENSATION AND EVAPORATION

In the special environment of a cave, the water vapor can both condense and evaporate on the rock surfaces. In both cases, this causes negative effects on the speleothems. Condensation works to corrode the calcite surfaces, and evaporation leaves flakes of calcite on the rock. Too much evaporation also creates stress on the bodies of the tiny glowworms. Since Waitomo Cave is visited by close to a half-million people a year, conditions need to be watched.

To see exactly how condensation happens—when, why, and where—in Waitomo Cave, researchers had to invent a new device. They decided upon a system of sets of parallel wires mounted flat. Condensation changes the electrical resistance between the wires. The device, hooked to electronic sensors, can then record the amount of condensation. Over a year of testing was required in three zones of the cave—the near-entrance, a transitional zone, and the most remote deep cave (the "Organ Pipe" area)—to see how conditions changed there and over all four seasons.

The results showed that condensation rates generally went up in daytime as the air temperature went up and in the warmer months (when it remains higher). In the transitional areas of the cave—the Cathedral and Banquet Chambers—the problem dropped gradually to zero in cooler months. At the Organ Loft, deep in the cave, though, condensation was always high and the moisture did not evaporate at all. And near the entrance, condensation and evaporation cycles occurred virtually all the time all yearlong. The researchers were able to tell cave officials roughly when to open and close the door and how long to leave it in either position, protecting the near-entrance and transitional areas, if not the Organ Loft, as much as possible.

Waitomo Cave, in New Zealand, is unusual in that it is home to forms of life not found in many areas outside of Asia. A limestone cave, it is rich in geologic variety also.

8

Carlsbad Cavern of New Mexico

United States

In the southeastern corner of New Mexico, about 15 miles (25 km) west of the town of Carlsbad, an extensive maze of caves lies hidden in the Guadalupe Mountains. Carlsbad Caverns is one of them, and it is part of a national park. At 1,027 feet (313 m) deep and 109,875 feet (33,490 m) long, Carlsbad is the ninth-deepest and the 15th-longest cave in the United States. It is yet more unusual than these numbers suggest, as will soon be described.

More than 65 other caverns have already been discovered near Carlsbad in this formation. Colorful names describe their intricacies: Christmas Tree, Corkscrew, Endless, Goat, Hell Below, Pink Dragon, Pink Panther, Spider, and Lechuguilla. The latter, dramatic and quite recently discovered, will receive more attention later in the chapter.) Geologists believe more caves are being formed in the Guadalupes—invisibly, of course—even today. The *water table*, below which caves like these always form, is now very deep here, about 600 feet (180 m) down. That makes it exceptionally hard to know what is going on at the cave-formation level.

The Carlsbad area is very dry at the surface. The Guadalupe Mountains run from this part of New Mexico into west Texas and south into Mexico, rising up from the Chihuahuan Desert. It is a vast expanse of nearly 47 million acres (19 million ha) of dry land.

Ancient, thick limestone reefs exist across the broad Carlsbad area, formed when this part of the country was underwater. Carlsbad is a limestone cave, cut into this stone, as are Mammoth Cave, the Cenotes, Lascaux, Sarawak Chamber, Waitomo, and Wind Cave, also covered in this book—though Carlsbad's formation comes with a twist, as will emerge. (See "Origin of the Landform: Caves" at the beginning of the book for perspective on the ways caves form.)

Geologists long considered Carlsbad Cavern puzzling—it is not exactly typical of a limestone cave. Among its oddities: Carlsbad has no *karst* landforms on the surface such as *sinkholes*. The natural cave entrances do not match where the water flowed, even long ago. The highest areas of the Guadalupe Mountains have few caves. In the area's many lower caves, the chambers tend to be immense and the passages between them often exceptionally high, relatively short, and abruptly ended. The caves tend to be very deep but not particularly long compared to their depth. They seem to close off quickly, at their deepest level, instead of continuing to grow visibly as the water table drops. These caves also hold massive blocks of gypsum (sometimes 32 feet [10 m] high) and also more native sulfur than would be expected. (Both are minerals.) An entire gypsum plain can also be seen at ground level in the desert. The Guadalupe caves are also among the most magnificently "decorated" caves in the world, with far more *speleothems* even than, say, Mammoth Cave. These formations have received names that hint at their appearance, including Proud Giants, Iceberg Room, Totem Pole, Papoose Room, and Statue of Liberty. Carlsbad also features nearly 9 million bats. To the trained eye and brain of a geologist, all this makes for a mystery—except, of course, the bats (they always know a good place to live when they find one).

ANCIENT FORMATION

Figuring out how Carlsbad Cavern formed begins with the basics of a limestone cave, the limestone. This stone is made of the collapsed and compacted bodies of sea creatures. The Carlsbad area began as a lowland in the *Precambrian* and *Cambrian* periods, about 600 million–460 million years ago. Flooding occurred in the late Cambrian and through the Mississippian period, when *tectonic* activity caused some sections of land in this area to uplift and some to sink. The ocean water that intruded brought in the sea creatures. By about 250 million years ago, they lived across an extent of about 400 miles (645 km), like Australia's Great Barrier Reef today. Along with these makings of the limestone, also developing were sandstone and dolomite. And some limestone zones were permeated with oil and natural gas.

By the end of the Permian, about 230 million years ago, the whole Carlsbad area was tilted and uplifted above sea level. The limestone reef areas began to become a series of dry, solid ridges, and much more of the formation became buried under salts evaporated from the ocean water and under gypsum rock.

Late in the *Cretaceous* period (about 65 million years ago), the sea flooded in again over a small part of the area. And over the entire period of 70–60 million years ago, groundwater was trickling down through the limestone. This launched the cave's formation. Beginning in the *Tertiary*

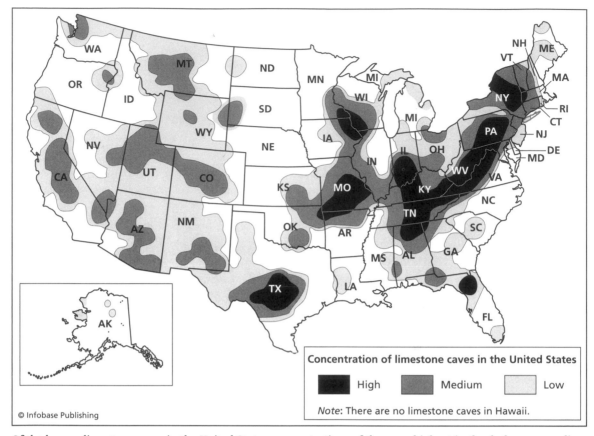

Concentration of limestone caves in the United States
High | Medium | Low
Note: There are no limestone caves in Hawaii.

© Infobase Publishing

Of the known limestone caves in the United States, concentrations of them are highest in the dark areas, medium in the gray zones (such as Carlsbad's), and fewest in the light gray areas.

about 10 million years ago, the area was uplifted again by the tectonic forces. And this uplift continues today across the American West. It has formed the great spine of the Rockies, not far from here.

Finally, in the *Pliocene-Pleistocene* period (3 million–1 million years ago), the Guadalupe Mountains had taken close to their present shape. The areas of limestone ridge became exposed *escarpments*. Carlsbad Cavern's ridge is some 787 feet (240 m) high and 1.5 miles (2.4 km) wide at its base.

As the rock uplifted to make these mountains, oil and natural gas had become concentrated in parts of the formation. Even today, this area is one of the largest oil- and natural gas–producing areas in the world.

OIL AND NATURAL GAS REACTIONS

When the broad limestone rock formation tilted further, the oil and natural gas gradually began to move through *faults* and *joints* in the rock. Oilfields, like most other places, have bacteria and other microbes. The ones that live in this underground terrain can exist without oxygen, feeding on the oil and natural gas and adding some of the excess energy to the sulfur in the gypsum rock. The reaction creates hydrogen sulfide gas.

Unlike water, which flows downward, hydrogen sulfide gas can easily migrate up, down, and sideways through rock. Here, some of it moved up to the water table. There it interacted with oxygen in the slightly salty water, along with whatever air was present. The result is sulfuric acid combined with groundwater. The native sulfur still present in the cave forms in this way also.

The sulfuric acid, highly corrosive, began to steadily dissolve the limestone. Left over from this process was carbonic acid, which also dissolves limestone, though less powerfully. (It is carbonic acid, formed as water drips down through surface soils, that is responsible for the formation of most limestone caves.) Both acids then migrated down, dissolved more rock, then abandoned that level on their way to the water table, which lowered as the cave formed. Remaining visible in a "hydrogen sulfide" cave like this one are blocks of gypsum.

Limestone caves are the most common kind of cave in the world, and most form through the carbonic acid dissolution. Not quite 10 percent form through the action of sulfuric acid the way Carlsbad has. It is this more powerful acid which was able to "eat" out the especially large chambers and passageways of Carlsbad Cavern. Its footprint can be easily seen in the Green Clay Room, for example, where bright-yellow sulfur deposits indicate the areas where the hydrogen sulfide mixed with oxygen.

The hydrogen sulfide process seems complete here, though carbonic acid is probably still working on the cave's rock at lower levels. In a few other areas of the world, though, as will be described in the "In the Field" section at the end of the chapter, hydrogen sulfide gas and sulfuric acid are still at work making caves. This is especially important since the gas is dangerous when encountered in enclosed spaces such as caves. Its hint is that it smells like rotten eggs.

WHEN THE CAVERNS FORMED

Caves within the Guadalupe Mountains formed at their greatest rates during two periods: 12–11 million years ago and 6–4 million years ago. These times probably coincided with periods of increased precipitation. Carlsbad's "Big Room" has been dated at about 4 million years, and the Green Clay Room at just slightly younger than that. At some point after this period, prehistoric animals began to use the cave—the bones of a large ground sloth, now extinct, have been found inside and dated at 29,700 years old.

Using degrees Celsius, this map shows U.S. cave temperature zones. The interior of a cave is usually equal to the year's average temperature at ground level above the cave.

THE BIG ROOM

Though Carlsbad Cavern has many dramatic areas, from the Left Hand Tunnel to the Bat Cave, the King's Palace to the Queen's Chamber, and the Devil's Den down to the lowest level Lake of the Clouds, the most amazing is probably the aptly named Big Room. It is the size of 14 football fields and could hold the whole U.S. Capitol building, standing up. The numbers: ca. 4,000 feet (1,219 m) long by 625 feet (191 m) wide, with a ceiling 255 feet (78 m) high. Tucked about 750 feet (230 m) below the surface, it is also the ninth-largest cave chamber in the world taken by surface area. One area within it is called the Bottomless Pit, another is the Jumping Off Place.

This chamber is flashier in color even than the orange-tan tones that predominate in other parts of Carlsbad Cavern. The Big Room features layers of cream-colored silt under yellow gypsum blocks; brick-red, brown, yellow, and tan silts; green clay; ochre-yellow, lemon-yellow, and pale-yellow native sulfur; and some pastel peach and purple deposits. The entrance to this chamber can be seen in the lower color insert on page C-6.

SPELEOTHEMS

The immense, intricate, and delicate cave formations that decorate Carlsbad Cavern have probably been growing for nearly 1 million years. Most, though, are fewer than 600,000 years old. Growth has occurred especially in humid periods aboveground, such as the periods of 600,000–300,000 years ago and 170,000–140,000 years ago. Only a small number of the cave's speleothems are still growing. Of these, some "rest" for 1,000 years. But the fastest-growing formation measured is enlarging at the rate of 160 cubic feet (4.5 m³) per year, which is very unusual. A couple of millimeters per year is more typical of speleothems growing in caves in general.

Earthquakes in the area over the eons have broken off some of the speleothems. But as long as water is dripping into a dry cave passageway or chamber, speleothems have the potential to grow.

Though the main cave rooms and halls here were cut out by sulfuric acid, most of the speleothems—and these are the most colorful ones—were made by the same, weaker carbonic acid that forms them in other limestone caves. It happens as various cave areas become dry except for the small drips and seepages. Some of the formations, though, were created by the sulfuric acid. Though the sulfate and gypsum are stable in most of the sulfuric acid speleothems, a few of these sulfate minerals can begin to dissolve even when people breathe on them. They are especially delicate speleothems.

Even the names of these formations are amazing: Texas toothpicks, popcorn, dogtooth spar, nailheads, gypsum flowers, cave clouds, cave balloons, cave rafts (they float on pools of water), moonmilk, soda straws (one here is 8.5 feet, or 2.5 m, long—immense for such a delicate feature), cave rope, the Giant Chandelier (which took approximately 800,000 years to reach its present size), tower coral, bell canopies, cave hair, cave pearls, lily pads, shields, cave blisters, snowballs, rosettes, helictites, coral pipes, cave flowers, needles, rims, frostwork, and cave cotton. The speleothems in Carlsbad are not only varied but also large, since the cave is old, built into rock with lots of faults and joints for the drips to find, and its chambers are huge. There has been plenty of room and plenty of time for them to form.

Most of Carlsbad's speleothems are white, orange, or transparent calcite. Some are made of aragonite (these tending more to needle shape), and some are carbonate. Colors of cream, pink, and orange pastel also occur commonly and come from crystallizations, trace metals, surface contaminants, and organic reactions even with bacteria in the rock. Some of these formations can be seen in the upper color insert on page C-7.

The Hall of Giants of Carlsbad Cavern got its name from the huge stalagmites. *(Harold W. Hoffman/Photo Researchers, Inc.)*

SPELEOTHEMS:
MOONMILK, POPCORN, CAVE PEARLS

The formation of the three cave "decorations" above gives a sampling of the chemistry of rock, microbes, and water in a limestone cave such as Carlsbad.

Moonmilk is a white paste, about the consistency of soft cream cheese. It is found here and there on the cave's walls. This speleothem is created as bacteria, actinomycetes, and other microbes break down wall rock and deposit mineral grains in the damp substance. Moonmilk is mainly calcite crystals and, here at Carlsbad, includes magnesium minerals such as hydromagnesite and huntite. Its name comes from the belief in the Middle Ages that it was formed by the rays of the Moon, passing through rock. (It is not.)

Popcorn, no more edible than moonmilk, looks like small white blobs. Carlsbad, lying under a desert, is naturally low in humidity. This means that evaporation of moisture happens quickly here. And in this situation, a very thin film of water, moving very slowly, builds formations, beginning with a bit of rock, then coating it layer by layer as the water slides over and leaves *precipitates*. This is similar in effect to the way a pearl forms inside an oyster shell. Popcorn generally grows on top of a larger speleothem.

Cave pearls are also similar to an oyster's pearls but in another way. The nucleus for this speleothem is a grain of sand or other mineral lying in a slightly concave bowl-shaped depression, one which happens to be under a drip coming down from the ceiling. The water gradually forms a small, shallow pool. Then as each new drip agigates the water, more mineral grains (occurring naturally in the water) are deposited on the nucleus "seed pearl." Cave pearls can range from pinhead, to marble-size, up to spheres as large as six inches (15 cm) in diameter. The movement of the water under the pearl keeps them from becoming solidly attached to the rock.

Cave pearls may seem rare now, even in The Rookery area of Carlsbad—originally named because so many "nests" of cave pearls there looked like birds' eggs—but they are not. They are, unfortunately, just easy for people to steal.

VISITING CARLSBAD

Though the cavern is in a desert environment, often scorchingly hot, inside Carlsbad it is always cool. The temperature hovers around 56°F (13°C) year-around. About 750,000 visitors a year enjoy the natural air conditioning here in the national park. Even more watch the two-hour bat flight out of the cave at dusk. These are Mexican frcc-tailed bats beginning their nocturnal hunt.

Six organized tours are offered, with two very short self-guided ones in addition. The main tours lead to the King's Palace (830 feet, or 253 m, down), Left Hand Tunnel, Slaughter Canyon Cave, Lower Cave, Hall of White Giant, and Spider Cave. One of the self-guided tours is to the Big Room, the other to the Natural Entrance. These trips range from 1.5 to four hours each. Some of them are civilized strolls down paved paths with electric lights toward a lunchroom, while others involve crawling on wet stone and through narrow passageways. Sites seen include *Permian*-age fossils, cave pools, and hundreds of speleothems, including cave pearls. Aboveground are diamondback rattlers, turkey vultures, and mountain lions.

LECHUGUILLA CAVE

Companion to Carlsbad Cavern, Lechuguilla Cave is about four miles (7 km) away. If possible, this cave is even more amazing. Lechuguilla is the deepest cave in the United States, plunging to 1,604 feet (489 m) down, as deep as a skyscraper of 160 stories is high. It is also the eighth longest. These numbers are always changing. Only about 90 miles (145 km) of its passages have been explored so far, and geologists estimate that there could be 200 miles (320 km) more of passages yet to be discovered in this cave. Its boundaries will probably soon go beyond those of the national park. Though the Lechuguilla entrance was known in 1914, the cave was not explored until the 1980s, well after Carlsbad.

Both caves are dark wildernesses, but Lechuguilla is warmer than Carlsbad, remaining at about 68°F (20°C) year-round, with 100 percent humidity. It is one of the most elaborately decorated caves in the United States, with a lot of cave popcorn, both green and blue underground pools with billowy cave rafts made of white stone, and myriad other speleothems. No mud or other debris clutters its broad, high passageways, though sharp-edged rocks, engulfing silence, and pits create the need for superb flashlights and careful walking.

None of Lechuguilla is open to the public, but an excellent way to experience it is by reading the mystery *Blind Descent*, by Nevada Barr. The author, a former National Parks Service ranger who has walked Lechuguilla, also includes a scene set in Carlsbad Cavern.

Areas of Lechuguilla have been kept closed off entirely so that microbiologists, astrobiologists, and other scientists can study the *extremophiles* inside. These ancient creatures are being researched, for example, for their potential in developing medicines and for the insight they may provide on whether life exists on Mars, Titan, and elsewhere in the solar system where extreme conditions also exist.

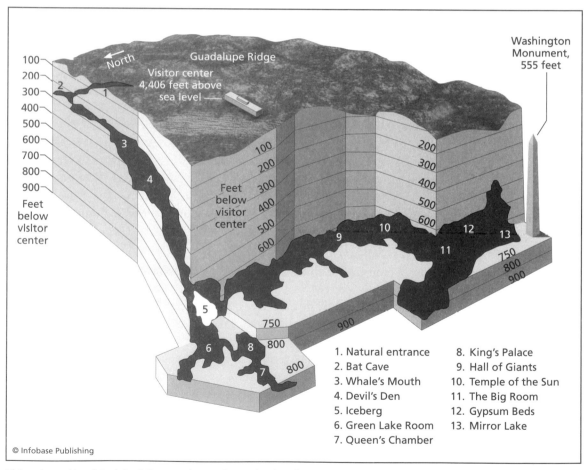

1. Natural entrance
2. Bat Cave
3. Whale's Mouth
4. Devil's Den
5. Iceberg
6. Green Lake Room
7. Queen's Chamber
8. King's Palace
9. Hall of Giants
10. Temple of the Sun
11. The Big Room
12. Gypsum Beds
13. Mirror Lake

© Infobase Publishing

This schematic of Carlsbad Cavern shows the main chambers and the levels of the cave in feet below the surface. Newer evidence now suggests that the cave descends even farther, down to 1,026 feet (313 m).

EXTREMOPHILES: WHERE THEY LIVE

As was mentioned earlier, some microscopic creatures inside Carlsbad live in and consume the oil and natural gas found in layers of the area's rock. Among these are extremophiles. After consuming these substances, they release electrons to the sulfur in the gypsum rock. This is what has created the hydrogen-sulfide gas that has corroded the rock to make Carlsbad Cavern and the other caves in the Guadalupe Mountains.

Other extremophiles eat some of the hydrogen-sulfide gas; yet others eat them; and still others emit methane after "breakfast." Yet more of them give caves their damp smell; others eat rocks (these, called lithotrophs, strip carbon from carbon dioxide gas in the rock); and still others are sealed into the calcite of cave formations. Extremophiles comprise a whole invisible food chain here and elsewhere on our planet.

On Earth, life requires carbon and energy and has found it in numberless variants. Oil and natural gas, originally dead vegetation, contain carbon just as surely as the grass does in the park, the vegetables do at the grocery, and our own bodies do. Our planet has myriad carbon-based life forms.

Extremophiles of a completely different kind have been found inside the salt crystals of Permian-era (270–225 million years ago) salts near Carlsbad Cavern. These extensive salt deposits date back to the time when the ancient seas evaporated here. If, as some scientists think, this salt has not recrystallized for 251 million years, these extremophiles, called halophiles, are that old. That would make them a million years older than the *Permian-Triassic* boundary. (If the salt has recrystallized, though, that would mean that the extremophiles could date back only as far as that event—it would have disrupted them.)

Though a cave such as Carlsbad is an extreme environment, almost a museum of darkness and rock, caves are not the only extreme location available for life to colonize. Extremophiles have also been found elsewhere: in suspended animation in 250-million-year-old glacial ice; in the deepest ocean trenches; in permafrost at least 32,000 years old and possibly elsewhere at 3 million years old in Siberia; in caustic hot springs such as those found in areas of Yellowstone and Iceland, at 250°F (120°C) temperatures; on volcanic vents in ocean bottoms, along tectonic plate boundaries, up to 235°F (113°C); as far down as 9,000 feet (2,745 m) in backyard soils; in oil wells as deep as 12,000 feet (3,700 m); in the presence of radiation that would kill anything else; in the wastewater of a mining operation, a sugar refinery, and an olive-processing plant; in salt deposits 10,000 feet (3,050 m) under the Mediterranean Sea; at thousands of feet (hundreds to thousands of meters) down in the basalt rock of the Columbia River Basin in the northwestern United States; in metals such as arsenic; and more than two miles (3 km) down in the world's deepest gold mine in South Africa.

The latter location, the workplace of some 5,000 miners and the research site for a few scientists, is near enough to the hot *core* of the planet that even powerful air conditioning depresses the temperature only down to 140°F (60°C). In a freshly cut area of rock, probably part of an ancient reef, the researchers found a rich trove of extremophiles, 100,000 up to 1 million of them per *gram* of rock. Some were eating iron oxide (rust), others consuming cobalt and uranium. The scientists' latest theory is that it is extremophiles (not only volcanically heated rock) that may actually concentrate the gold in a gold mine. This is what makes it worth mining. It is beginning to emerge in science that processes once thought to be inorganically chemical can actually be biochemical, directed by tiny creatures like extremophiles.

EXTREMOPHILES: WHAT THEY CAN DO FOR HUMANS

Though the lives of these creatures have their own rationale (every life-form has its place), what they do can also be very useful to humans. Some are yielding new antibiotics. One of the sulfur organisms makes B vitamins as a by-product. Several kinds consume toxic wastes, such as the organic solvents benzene and octane used in gasoline. These should also prove quite useful in treating sewage and other effluents, just as they have been already in mining dumps. Other extremophiles actually create the organic solvents. Some of these creatures are used as lab enzymes to accomplish useful chemical reactions. Others may be yielding a new way to make ethanol, a plant-based gasoline substitute. Some consume carbon monoxide, too, a gas fatal to people. Since extremophiles are a new area of scientific research—one with plenty of room for scientists of the future—much more will surely be discovered.

For more about extremophiles, please see the sections under this name in chapters 1, 2, 3, 9, and 10.

EXTREMOPHILES: FIRST LIFE ON EARTH?

These creatures have probably lived on Earth for several billion years. Why do scientists think so? It is because the early Earth, formed about 4.6 billion years ago from scorching hot gases and minerals—and without oxygen—was itself an extreme environment. It was just the place creatures such as these would have flourished, and now it matches their current homes.

Many readers have probably heard the expression "life came from the sea." It probably did, and about 4 billion years ago—but it did not crawl out in the form of a fully formed frog or other such organism. Most likely, organic acids oozed out like scum onto land, finding the carbonic acid of the first rainfalls to build the first soils. This ooze may even have made rocks, a bit the way sea creatures make coral today. All this set the stage for land life. The makers of those original organic acids were the extremophiles.

CAVE FISH

Fish that live all their lives in caves—as a *troglobite* species—are rare. Fewer than 10 such species are known across the United States. Scientists believe that all of them were originally swept into the caves by flooding rivers at the time of the glacial melt and in ordinary floods since then. The ones that survived inside were probably those which had inhabited dimmer places in their aboveground lives, such as under the stones in creeks or in thick streambed vegetation. These fish were able to find food in conditions of low light.

The fish that live in caves now are blind, and their body color is pale or even translucent. Some lack eyelids, some lack optic nerves completely, while others have some optic nerve material in place though not usable. Cave fish also tend to have sensors on their skin that are especially sensitive to vibrations in the water, longer antennae, bigger jaws, more teeth, and more taste buds. Almost all these species are fewer than four inches (10 cm) long. In their caves, they use vibrations to find their mates and food, which is ample though not in huge supply. These fish thrive in the stable temperatures and high relative humidity of a cave—and in the utter darkness.

How have cave fish made such extensive adaptations to life in an environment hardly ideal for fish? And in little time? No cave fish species has been found in caves covered by glacial ice in the most recent period of glaciation—and that ended just 15,000–10,000 years ago across the United States. The time since then is not a long time period for evolution to create such huge differences. After all, readers who taped their eyes shut for a day, or 10 years, or 100 years, would not find that their eyes had disappeared and their vision vanished.

The evolutionary processes that led to these unusual fish did take time, many generations of time. But a generation in a fish is no more than one year. So, each year, the baby fish born whose vision was worse and whose skin was lower in colorful camouflage did no worse than their siblings at reaching adulthood and bearing young in the cave. They did not do better, they just did not do worse. The selection process by which some creatures in a group thrive or die—called natural selection—rewards characteristics that benefit survival, such as greater sensing of vibrations, and does not reward what is no longer useful. And good vision is not being rewarded if it does not lead to more offspring. So a population of fish developed that included those whose eyesight was poor and camouflage faint, but that, for example, had better sensory receptors.

Small genetic fluctuations, called mutations, are regularly occurring in the genetic code of any species. Most of these are bad, some are neutral, and some are good for a species. Fish with mutations that led to worse vision would not do well in an ordinary river—they would probably die. But not here. And, gradually, more and more of their offspring, also with poor vision like their parent(s), began to inhabit the cave. In stages like this, the fish species became blind. The same process worked for their pale or translucent coloration, also gradually.

Another factor helped the process along immensely. It seems that only a small group of genes is needed to make the transformation to blind and pale. And the very same two genes that lead to loss of eyes lead to bigger jaws and more taste buds. It is easy to see why this amazing process of evolution, actually jerry-built, is considered a directed miracle by some people.

The first extremophiles may well have arrived on the early Earth within the carbonaceous chrondrite meteorites that pounded the planet. As the solar system was forming, Earth was pummeled almost constantly by meteorites, including this kind, which is now the rarest. Carbonaceous chrondrites, as one can guess from their name, contain carbon, organic carbon materials (up to 5 percent by weight), nitrogen, and sometimes a trace of water. A meteorite of this type did hit the Earth in 1969, and analysis of it showed carbon and several amino acids. An earlier such sample contained more than 75 amino acids. That is about all it takes for life to develop.

And, if this scenario of new life unfolded here, might not similar events have played out on Mars, Titan, and elsewhere? Maybe even everywhere? Where else might this process be going on today? Is there an "Earth" close to forming life in a neighboring part of our galaxy right now? And are any of the same ancient species of extremophiles, rained down inside meteorites still thriving in our extreme environments today? Scientists such as geochemists are investigating questions like this actively.

IN THE FIELD:
HYDROGEN SULFIDE CAVES ELSEWHERE

Though this kind of cave formation process is not rare in the Guadalupe Mountains—because of the proximity of the vast deposits of oil and natural gas in the extensive limestone reefs—it is unusual worldwide. Geologists have studied hydrogen sulfide caves around Fiumo Vento in Italy, Akhali Atoni in the Caucasus Mountains near the Black Sea, Movile Cave in Romania, Lower Kane Cave in Wyoming (near the Montana border), and in a handful of other places.

Lower Kane, only about the size of a typical subway station, seems to be an actively forming hydrogen sulfide cave today. As such, it is a magnet for scientists willing to squeeze down through a 30-inch- (75-cm-) wide crack and don gas masks to protect against the toxic gases.

Here, they have found three hot spring–fed pools bubbling out hydrogen sulfide gas, on which float slimy, stringy living mats, vivid in acid orange, murky blue-black, bright purple, and white. Are these creatures enhancing the acid attacks that have pitted the walls of Lower Kane Cave? Scientists began their tests with DNA analysis of some of the many kinds of organisms here, and some of them layered in the mats turned out to be extremophiles, in addition to bacteria. New species were discovered, as almost always happens when extremophiles are studied.

The researchers also developed a simple method to see if the extremophiles in Lower Kane Cave were indeed engaged in active cave construction. They suspended two plastic tubes in the gassy pools, both holding chips of limestone, the bedrock of the cave. One tube was topped with a basic plastic mesh, open enough that both water and extremophiles could enter it and move among the limestone chips. The second tube had a membrane through which only water could enter. Both tubes were left in place for several months.

Then, under a microscope, the scientists looked for wear and tear on the limestone. In the first tube, the only one in which the extremophiles had been able to operate, the limestone was indeed corroded. The second tube had no such evidence of action. Hence, wherever the extremophiles of Lower Kane encountered the cave's limestone, they could hollow out more cave.

Carlsbad Cavern is relatively unusual among limestone caves in that the chemical agent carving out the cave was sulfuric acid. The result is, in addition, an amazing place.

9

Wind Cave of South Dakota

United States

Wind Cave is buried in South Dakota's southwestern corner, close to both the Wyoming and Nebraska borders and to the town of Custer City. Its aboveground terrain is the southern Black Hills, the most eastern outcrop of the Rocky Mountains. Here, in the foothills, the forests of the higher elevations meet the grasslands of the lower lands. Above Wind Cave thrive bison herds, bobcats, prairie dogs, pronghorns, and elk.

Wind Cave's entrance lies sloped, set on a canyon floor. Near the opening live bushy-tail wood rats, deer mice, tiger salamanders, frogs, various snakes, various insects, and, of course, bats. The cave was known to the native Indians, entered by settlers in 1881, and has been a national park since 1903.

Wind Cave's name comes from the stiff winds that can be encountered *inside* the cave. This feature, as well as the amazing mazelike layout of its passageways and its unusual boxwork *speleothem*, will be discussed as the chapter proceeds. The cave is also unusual in that its average annual temperature—53°F (11.7°C)—is significantly greater than the average annual temperature aboveground. Scientists think that this indicates a *tectonic* heat source. And indeed this area has minimal to moderate tectonic activity, as evidenced by the occasional earthquake.

Wind Cave is long, the sixth longest in the world. Its length, as surveyed so far, adds up to 116.06 miles (186.8 km) of twisted, straight, and closed-loop paths. A few more miles of these are surveyed by volunteer cavers every year. Using the wind's force as a clue, scientists estimate that only about 2 percent of the cave's volume (its air volume) has been discovered. Once Wind Cave is fully mapped, it will almost certainly extend beyond the boundaries of the national parkland.

The cave is also deep. Its deepest pit plunges 528 feet (161 m) down. And lakes on the lowest level lie 654 feet (199.3 m) below Wind Cave's highest point.

ANCIENT ORIGINS

A limestone cave, Wind Cave was cut into one of the oldest limestone formations on the planet. The thick limestone here formed 340–330 million years ago. As usual, this common cave-forming bedrock is evidence of an ancient arm of ocean—here part of the ancestral Pacific extended into the area—since limestone rock is the compacted bodies and shells of sea creatures. (For more on limestone caves, please see chapters 1, 2, 3, 4, 7, and 8.

By about 320–310 million years ago, the first *sinkholes* and caves were forming in this new *karst terrain*. Sands, gravels, muds, silts, and clays that were deposited in layers helped to give the new limestone cave its strata and support, since these rocks are less porous than the limestone. The area was much less arid in those days than it is today, allowing these new materials to wash in and over the terrain.

By the late *Jurassic*, 155–147 million years ago, dinosaurs roamed aboveground here. Mountains had grown to the west (they have long since worn down), and these peaks intercepted the rain clouds. This made the area quite arid, in an atmospheric phenomenon called a *rainshadow*. Streams flowing downhill from the mountain did fill underground *aquifers*, however. A large saline lake existed in the area also. The Wind Cave terrain still has ample aquifers, and evidence of them is reflected in Wind Cave—more than 10 percent of the monitoring stations inside the cave are near to water. Among the lakes inside the cave that have been given names are Phantom Lake, Windy City Lake, and Lovely Little Lake.

At about 141 million years ago, the end of the Jurassic, the limestone depositing was complete here. The climate was warm in those days—scientists think that even the Arctic and Antarctic were ice-free. So no long winters interfered with the seepage of rainwater through soils, the process by which limestone caves form.

From approximately 40 million to a half-million years ago, the cave took on its present shape and extent. The *water table* fell, and the upper levels of the cave dried. Speleothems began to form in the dry levels. Sediments exposed in the cave today have been dated to 2 million years ago.

MAZE CAVE

Though Wind Cave is extremely long, much of its length is a maze of loops, dead-ends, and twisted passageways. A labyrinth, it is considered the most complex three-dimensional maze of any cave in the world. All of its known extent is compressed into a space which at the surface is only about one mile by 1.25 miles (1.6 km by 2 km).

A maze cave differs from a stream cave, with the latter much more common. A stream cave is shaped like the branches and twigs of a tree, with passageways ending in a wall rather than circling back.

BREATHING CAVES, BLOWING CAVES, WIND CAVE

Wind is not at all uncommon in caves, though it is usually so light that it can be hard to detect, except by instruments. Cavers do learn to use the wind, however, to find undiscovered passageways. When they feel a faint wind on their faces from behind a loose barrier of boulders or a rough blockage of gravel, they know to tunnel in to search for more cave. In Wind Cave, however, the winds can be powerful enough to blow a piece of paper right out of a person's hand—up to 75 miles per hour (120 km/hr)! Park officials have installed a revolving door now, bringing the maximum wind speed down to "only" about 60 miles per hour (97 km/hr).

Cave winds occur when barometric pressure outside the cave drops and air inside the cave moves out to equalize it. This is a version of what happens if an airplane door blows off a plane in flight. (The cabins are pressurized so that passengers can breathe, but the air outside is very thin. The cabin air rushes out to equalize it—and with enough force to take a non-seatbelted passenger out with it.

Barometric pressure aboveground changes with the time of day. Every night, the barometer rises slightly, as the air cools and becomes denser, encouraging air flow into the cave. The next morning, as the air pressure falls again when the air warms, air flows out of the cave. This happens to some degree at every cave that has an open entrance, more noticeably near these entrance(s). Of course, the process takes a long time to move the air masses that fill a whole cave.

"Breathing caves" are a special case in which the air seems to flow in for a few minutes, then pause, and next move out again for about the same length of time. This happens when the shape of the cave's passages forms a "neck" for the air. It is as though someone were blowing across the neck of a bottle. Usually it is just one T-shaped area of the cave that does this "breathing."

"Blowing caves" are another variant. These caves have two entrances, with one higher than the other. In a kind of fireplace chimney effect, one entrance or the other spouts out air. This is usually a seasonal phenomenon. Colder air enters the lower entrance in winter, and it is warmed up once inside the cave. It then rises, as warm air always does, to exit at the higher entrance. The directions are reversed in summertime. The cave with the most pronounced chimney-effect wind is Pinargozu Cave in Turkey—103.33 miles per hour (166.3 km/hr) of wind speed.

The most dramatic changes in air pressure occur as a major storm approaches any cave aboveground. The barometer is dropping, sometimes dramatically. This definitely occurs in the Great Plains of South Dakota, and readers may have seen pictures of the huge thunderheads in prairie storms. This kind of weather makes Wind Cave especially windy.

Historians think major winds like these allowed the Indians to discover the cave. It is certainly how it was discovered by the settlers in 1881.

VISITING WIND AND JEWEL

When the door is opened, visitors immediately realize how Wind Cave got its name. Five tours lead inside by stairs and elevator to areas called the Fairgrounds and the Garden of Eden. These last from an hour to four hours. One of them, the Wild Cave Tour, involves mostly crawling, while another is done by candlelight. Others are on flat paths well lit by electricity, as can be seen in the lower color insert on page C-7.

Nearby Jewel Cave can also be visited. It is a major cave in length and depth, at 130 miles (209 km) long and 587 feet (179 m) deep. This makes it the third longest in the world, outdoing even Wind Cave. Though its name comes from its jewel-like calcite crystal speleothems, it is also windy. Some areas of Jewel Cave have been clocked at 32 miles per hour (51 km/hr) of wind speed, not as dramatic as Wind Cave's but still quite impressive.

Scientists believe that more caves, now completely unknown, probably exist in the area too. They are waiting to be discovered.

This speleothem, called frostwork, looks like snow or gauze but is made of rock. *(National Park Service)*

SPELEOTHEMS

An ornate array of cave formations has been growing in Wind Cave for about 500,000 years. And this cave is exceptional for its variety of speleothems. (For background on how they form in general, see chapters 1 and 2 as well as sections elsewhere in the book with "speleothems" in their title.)

Speleothem types here include cave flowers, starbursts, dogtooth and nailhead spar, Christmas trees, button popcorn, frostwork, sawtooth flowstone, *stalactites*, *stalagmites*, boxwork, and helictite bushes. Almost all here are variants of calcite crystals, with a small percentage built of gypsum crystals. The latter two speleothems will be described in the next section.

The rooms in which these formations are found have been given equally vivid names: Figure Eight Room, Chamber of Lost Souls, Club Room, Fairy Palace, Pearly Gates, Elephant Trunk, Silent Lake, Xerox Room, Post Office, Second Crossroads, and many others. As with the names of the speleothems, these reflect efforts to describe their appearance for visitors.

SPELEOTHEMS: BOX WORK

Perhaps the most noticeable cave formation in Wind Cave is known as box work, with an example included in the upper color insert on page C-8. Other caves feature this speleothem, but it is probably here that the most elaborate and abundant versions exist.

Box work is built as slender shards of calcite are extruded from cracks in the cave's walls and ceiling, these cracks just inches or centimeters or fractions of inches apart. Forming a latticework eventually, as the blades intersect at various angles, the result looks like the inside layer of a corrugated cardboard box.

Geologists still do not completely understand how box work forms. But it is possible that stressed gypsum rock (which had dried, dampened, and dried again) provides the original wall and ceiling cracks. The cracks form in the right shapes to force the calcite into its blades. Then the intervening rock material is dissolved away, throwing everything into further bas-relief.

SPELEOTHEMS: HELICTITE BUSHES

At least as amazing as the box work formations are delicate, seemingly gravity-defying constructions known as helictite bushes. One of Wind Cave's helictites bushes is probably in the top five for size of any cave's in the world. It is a "bush" about six feet (1.8 m) high, three feet (.9 m) wide, and two feet (.6 m) front to back. More typical helictites are less than a foot (.3 m) long and twisted into snakelike shapes. All are made of extremely narrow tubes of rock.

Delicate helictite bushes like these are unusually common in Wind Cave. *(National Park Service)*

Helictite bushes seem to form when the dripping water, necessary to create all speleothems, happens to move so slowly that actual drops never form. Instead, a thin film of fluid flows out to reach the tip of the formation. There, in thin layer by thin layer, the minerals in the water *precipitate* out, crystallizing in an irregular fashion. Deformation of each crystal, which makes it unequally balanced and so not pointed straight down, then twists the growing helictites gradually, crystal by crystal. The mineral crystals may be deforming through other processes also and are still under study. But it is known that helictites form in especially dry areas of caves where the water slips along rather than drips.

SPELEOTHEMS AND EVAPORATION

The amount of dripping water affects the size of all speleothems. And though Wind Cave has plenty of interior water, from the underground aquifers mentioned earlier, its water evaporates more readily than in most areas. This is because of the significant wind. During the long, cold winters here when the air aboveground holds very little moisture—and if the cave's entrance is open—about 16 gallons (73 L) of water in the form of water vapors exits the cave via the wind, every hour. Given that dryness, the size and profusion of the speleothems in Wind Cave is quite amazing. It reflects the length of time that they have been building and the fact that the aquifers make water available.

ENVIRONMENTAL ISSUES

The Black Hills area where Wind Cave lies holds ample aquifers, as was mentioned earlier. These are used for drinking water. The limestone formation is also well cracked, or fractured. This situation creates the potential for contaminants to enter the water supply, since they can percolate down from the surface and move in the groundwater along the many fractures.

EXTREMOPHILES: THE RANGE OF THESE CREATURES

These ancient organisms come with many names, reflecting their biological niches. There are hyperthermophiles, which love the extreme heat of geothermal vents, boiling mud pits, and the inner zones of volcanoes; about 50 species of these have been identified so far. There are also piezo-psychrophiles, which live at immensely high pressures under the ocean and cannot tolerate light. "Regular" psychrophiles also exist; their favorite temperature is 59°F (15°C), and they die if warmed up. And acidophiles love the sulfur of volcanic fluids or sulfur veins in caves.

Many extremophiles are anaerobic, living in conditions without oxygen. This group—a cross-category that includes species within all the types mentioned in the previous paragraph—can exist at a temperature range from about 41°F to 230°F (5°C to 110°C). These are certainly versatile creatures.

RECENT SCIENTIFIC DISCOVERIES AT WIND CAVE

In addition to discovering and surveying more areas of the cave each year, scientists and volunteer cavers have made other discoveries over the last five years or so. The following list is adapted from the Wind Cave National Park Web site, where readers can check for even newer findings posted:

- A new, flexible kind of box work, made out of a type of clay, was found.
- An old cave entrance, which had been filled in, was discovered.
- A new lake was located.
- A natural cave passage was discovered just five feet (1.5 m) below a sidewalk. It is near enough to the surface to hold water after a heavy rain.
- A speleothem called gypsum rope was found, about 14 inches (35.5 cm) long, and the room in which it is located was given a new name: Golden Rope Room.
- Several new openings were located that leak air from the cave to the surface.
- Woodrats were seen 80 feet (25 m) below the surface, nowhere near an entrance.
- Fossilized *extremophiles* were found, of the type which consume iron. (Other extremophile species have also been found in the cave.)

Not all extremophiles are Archaea, the most ancient creatures on the planet. Some have evolved much more recently. But, speaking broadly, these creatures are a living museum, a reflection of the nature of the early Earth: hot, sulfurous, acidic, salty, alkaline, and without oxygen. This is where they evolved, and this is where they have found it possible to live today, in the extreme terrains remaining. Caves are among these.

EXTREMOPHILES ON THE FRONTIER

These creatures are considered an exciting area of scientific research because they tend to be so primitive—and also because they can be useful to humans. Some can be pressed into service as "instant wetlands," removing toxins from storm water that would otherwise flow into lakes, ponds, streams, and rivers. Some concentrate valuable metals out of rocky metallic ores into valuable metals. One kind is used to clean contact lenses, others to create enzymes useful in making detergents and paper. Others make fructose (fruit sugar) or cheese. Some extremophiles are even themselves edible. They can double the size of their colonies in anywhere from 10 minutes up to a few hours. They are indeed at the frontier of science. For more on them, please see the sections with their names in the book's other chapters.

IN THE FIELD: CAVE SURVEYING

Those who wonder if they will ever use trigonometry in daily life need wonder no more. This math is used every time a new area of a cave like Wind Cave is surveyed by volunteers. Tens of thousands of passages have been plotted here so far, each also requiring the use of a compass, an inclinometer (to measure the tilt of a stretch of cave), rolls of tape, and a notebook made of mylar (regular paper tends to turn limp and soggy in a cave). These methods work well, while Global Positioning System (GPS) technology cannot "see" underground. In this technology, signals are bounced off satellites to determine geographic positions.

Thousands and thousands of areas are left to survey in Wind Cave by those willing to put on a head lamp, scramble over boulders, creep through narrow places, take notes, draw the shapes of passages in the dark, and use that trig. Volunteer caver teams are doing this every year. A small, numbered marker, also made of mylar, is left in the cave every time they finish an area, to note where one surveyed area ends and a new one will begin. These are called the "stations" of the cave.

The compass is used to note whether a given cave passage heads north, south, east, or west. The inclinometer registers its vertical angle as the passage rises or dips. The height of the passage is also measured and key speleothems noted. All these measurements are recorded on a graph and other forms.

These results, though useful, present only a sloped distance, not the same as a horizontal distance. This is where the trigonometry comes in: Horizontal distance = slope distance × the cosine of the inclination; also, to get the depth of each area relative to the rest of the cave, rise (between this one and the last station) = slope distance × the sine of the inclination. The teams do this math once aboveground.

When these equations have been solved for an individual cave station, those numbers can be compared to those from stations analyzed previously. The calculations are done relative to the point that is the cave's entrance, called a benchmark. The results yield a three-dimensional measure of the cave. To see the process in action, go to the Wind Cave National Park Web site and click on "Cave Surveying."

IN THE FIELD:
GEOGRAPHIC INFORMATION SYSTEMS

Even with careful surveying enhanced by trigonometry, it is difficult to orient the cave to the aboveground features, and it is especially hard to know how deep the cave lies under a given surface location, beneath all the thick surface soil and tangled upper-level passages. A maze cave, Wind Cave is packed into a compact area like a lot of macaroni pressed down into a small barrel by a heavy lid. Orientation vis-à-vis the surface is important because parking lots, sewage facilities, and proposed housing developments may lie or be proposed to lie above the cave. They could drain effluents into it.

Beginning with the information from Wind Cave's 150 survey stations, per kilometer, geologists have added the use of Geographic Information Systems (GIS) to integrate all the belowground survey data into three-dimensional maps and combine it with surface data from GPS. Software is necessary to mesh this surface topography with the interior survey data.

Though this technique is only a few years old here, it has already provided new hypotheses. Wind Cave may extend even farther beyond park boundaries than was thought before. It may even connect to Jewel Cave some 20 miles (30 km) away, by either air-filled or water-filled passageways.

Some GIS data have already been used to protect the cave and add to the cave experience. The parking lot has been remodeled to better absorb and direct rainwater away from the cave (since this water always includes gas, oil, tire particles, and the like). Sewage treatment facilities have been moved. And herbicides, directed at nonnative, invasive plant species aboveground, have been kept from dripping down into the cave with the rain. Visitors can now even take a virtual "tour" of the cave entirely aboveground.

Wind Cave is known for its box work speleothems (as can be seen in the upper color insert on page C-8) and for the fact that the structure of the cave itself creates wind. It is so complex that more of the cave is being discovered regularly.

10

Kverkfjöll Cave of the Vatnajökull Glacier

Iceland

Hidden in the Vatnajökull, the largest glacier in the world outside of the Arctic and Antarctica, are tunnels and caves carved out of solid ice. The carving is done by rivers and by geothermal activity, the deep heat of the planet that reaches close to the surface in Iceland. The most famous cave, Kverkfjöll, is about 1.8 miles (2.9 km) long, plunges to 1,722 feet (525 m) below the glacier's surface, and has three entrances. Also cut into the Vatnajökull's north and northeast white expanse are additional tunnels. They exist within the Eyjabakkajökull area and along the Grimsfjall rim of the Grimsvötn volcano (which lies

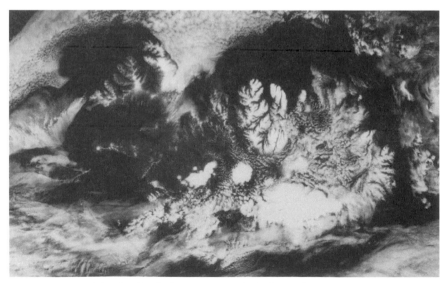

In this NASA aerial of Iceland, the Vatnajökull glacier is the large white mass in the country's southeast. *(NASA/Visible Earth)*

under the glacier). Some of the country's smaller glaciers conceal yet more such tunnels. None of the cave tunnel complexes at the base of the Vatnajökull have been fully explored. The name for these formations is *glacier cave*, not *ice cave*, since the latter term refers to rock caves with significant ice inside.

Some of the glacial rivers in the Vatnajökull area also drain geothermal areas under the glacier. The melted glacier water then enlarges the tunnels even more, allowing cavers to enter during the warmer seasons. This is the situation at Kverkfjöll, while other caves such as those within Tungnaárjökull and Eyjafjallajökull glaciers elsewhere are only accessible during winter when the glacial water is minimal and not in the way. Ice caves and tunnels such as these change throughout the year, freezing up, "remodeling," and so on.

Ice cave and tunnel complexes change their dimensions within a year, between years, even over a single day. A warm summer afternoon brings more warmth—and meltwater. Some can even collapse quickly, since the weight of the glacier above them is immense.

The Vatnajökull glacier of Iceland covers 10–11 percent of the country, an otherwise green country about the size of Kentucky that is situated over dark lava. (The old expression, "Greenland is ice, and Iceland is green," is quite true.) At about 3,150 square miles (8,160 km²), this glacier is slapped over a vast, high plateau, with its highest area at 4,200–6,100 feet (1,280–2,119 m) above sea level. The Vatnajökull also throws down about 40 "paws," or lobes, into various valleys; some of these are quite easy to climb up on, at least for short distances. Depending upon topography, and the volume of water between the slippery bottom layer of ice and the ground, these lobes move downhill at rates from four inches (10 cm) per day up to 3.28 feet (1 m) per day. (A few of them experience a huge surge every few decades.)

Glacial caves are not at all simple to explore, though their beauty is mesmerizing. Of course they are slippery and sometimes quite steep, making a fall fatal. Naturally, they are also very cold. But the less obvious factor is a possible movement of the ice. Chunks of ice the size of refrigerators can break off suddenly from the walls of these caves. This can happen when pressure from the ice, moving so slowly as to be undetectable by cavers, squeezes a wall permeated by cracks, or when the glacier itself flexes slightly. Even a small chunk of catapulting ice could break a caver's arm or leg, causing a disastrous stumble. Larger ones are obviously yet more problematic. Warmer weather can destabilize the entire shell of the cave, too, since that can mean running water, perhaps hidden from view. Glacier caves are actually safer to explore in winter, though here in Iceland it would be too hazardous to try to reach them then.

There are more considerations also. Exploring Kverkfjöll requires carrying in breathing equipment similar to that used by scuba divers. This is necessary since passages of this cave can become high in sulfur dioxide and carbon dioxide in the form of steamy fumes. Other required gear includes a waterproof suit, crampons, ice axes, rappelling gear—and plenty of nerve. In spite of all this, spring and summer adventure tours are available into the Kverkfjöll glacier cave for intrepid visitors. (For an interior view of the cave, see the lower color insert on page C-8.)

FORMATION OF KVERKFJÖLL

A glacier cave's formation begins with the nature of the glacier itself. Glaciers are always moving to some degree, since their greater mass is pressing downhill at higher elevations. They slip along on the thin layer of melted water between the ice mass and the ground. (The water melts at the bottom of a glacier because ground is warmer than ice.) Their movement may be an invisibly slow creep or perhaps a surge.

The glacier's movement creates cracks in the ice called fissures. Some are deep and wide, others knife-blade thin. Into and through these fissures can flow running water, especially in summer when the top layer of the glacier is exposed to the warmer Sun.

Fissures also occur from land tides. Readers surely realize that the Moon's gravity tugs at the oceans to create tides there. But the Moon is also pulling at the land. Though land, and whatever is on it—such as a glacier—can be tugged at much less readily than a body of water, land does indeed move slightly. This adds to the number of fissures in the ice. That creates yet more places for meltwater to flow. Gradually, the water expands some of the cracks enough that they widen into caves.

Kverkfjöll has yet another cave-creating force: hot springs. Iceland is a highly volcanic place, much like Hawaii, and heat from deep within the Earth here can be very close to the surface in places. This is true even when no actual volcano is erupting nearby. The hot springs cause bubbling water and sulfur dioxide gas in all seasons under the Vatnajökull glacier near Kverkfjöll, and their heat and the meltwater created are the chief architects of this cave. Because of these hot springs, Kverkfjöll does not freeze back into solid ice every winter. It remains a glacier cave, though a smaller one and differently shaped.

AGE OF THE CAVE

No one knows the exact age of Kverkfjöll and the other glacier caves of Vatnajökull. These caves were not even explored until the 1980s. But it is known that the Vatnajökull itself formed as a glacier beginning only about 2,500 years ago—during a cold, wet climatic period when snow built up and did not melt much even in the summer. As the snow layers compressed, they became solid ice. The glacier here was probably fully formed by about 2,000 years ago. This makes its glacier caves very young compared to the limestone caves in the book.

It may seem surprising that the Vatnajökull is not leftover ice from the most recent Ice Age, the period of glaciation that ended in the United States about 10,000 years ago and in Iceland about 9,000 years ago. But nothing like the Vatnajökull existed at that point, though there were ice masses at high elevations.

During the broader Ice Age, the *Pleistocene*, Iceland was entirely under ice. The country is still bouncing back from this experience, literally. The process is called *isostatic rebound*. The land, once pressed down by the immense weight of the ice, then released when it retreats, rises back up. The rate, less than an inch (2.54 cm) per year here now, is too small to observe directly. But in southeast Iceland, a town called Höfn is watching its harbor close off as the land gradually is rising in this way. The harbor will not close completely, geologists say, but it is already a less secure and less convenient shape for the town's fishing fleet (its major livelihood).

The town of Höfn is adjacent to the Vatnajökull, which is shrinking now, very gradually. That means isostatic rebound will continue to proceed here in the areas from which the glacier vanishes. Kverkfjöll, significantly farther to the north, and on the higher-elevation north side of the glacier, is not yet affected by this and will not be for a very long time.

UNDER THE GLACIER: VOLCANIC ERUPTIONS

The volcanic nature of Iceland is quite pronounced, since a volcano erupts somewhere there every four or five years. A full seven of these volcanoes lie concentrated under the ice of the Vatnajökull glacier. Even the immense weight of a major glacier cannot keep a volcano from erupting.

Over the last 1,100 years, about 80 eruptions have occurred under Kverkfjöll's parent glacier. None has been closer than about 18.5 miles (30 km) from this glacier cave, but eruptions have had impressive effects (no one would want to be in a glacier cave when a volcano was erupting, even faraway). The ice becomes stressed by the force of the eruption over a large expanse. And large stream cavities can form within the ice as the heat from the lava melts it. Both effects make large areas of the glacier less stable. Chunks of the lava often force themselves into the ice, too, cooling there into columns. (This columnar basalt, as it forms an aboveground cave, is described in chapter 6, Fingal's Cave of Scotland, Great Britain.) Further reasons for paying attention to Iceland's volcanoes, via its elaborate volcano-monitoring system, will emerge as the chapter progresses.

UNDER THE GLACIER: A 1996 ERUPTION

An eruption in 1996, under the northwestern part of the Vatnajökull glacier, about 18.5 miles (30 km) from Kverkfjöll, has been studied in considerable detail. The event was monitored over the entire period of eruption by remote-control instruments and by plane flyovers.

The eruption, occurring over 13 to 14 days in the fall of 1996, involved two volcanoes simultaneously, Bardarbunga and Grimsvötn. Both volcanoes maintain *calderas* filled with water under the glacier, since tectonic heat is more or less constant here. And Grimsvötn has erupted six times in the last 100 years. The eruption was at first invisible, though geologists knew it was happening—*seismographs* in the area registered deep-wave quivers and disruptions here and as far as 12.5 miles (20 km) away from the two hidden volcanoes. But, after about two days, evidence emerged at the surface. Depressions shaped like large bowls formed and gradually filled with meltwater. By the next day, the ice surface was hissing steam. Over the next few days, steam, ash, and *tephra* broke through the glacial "lid"—the 1,476-foot- (450-m-) thick ice in the area—and was shooting more than six miles (10 km) into the air. Black lava "bombs" began to litter the white ice, also. During this time, *magma* (flowing lava) was being forced sideways into the ice and into the ground as well as up into the glacier above the eruption.

THE CAVES OF GREENLAND

Greenland is almost completely covered by ice. Though its glacial masses, like the Vatnajökull's, are thinning and shrinking around the edges in the Earth's current period of climate change, Greenland still has plenty of potential for glacier caves. The two-mile- (3.2-km-) thick ice at higher elevations slides down toward the sea in all directions, at an average rate here of a few inches per year, creating significant fissures as the glacier moves. By summertime each year, caves are forming. Summer meltwater begins to carve them out, finding all the fissures and gathering strength until it becomes rushing rivers.

The caves all begin from the top down here, since Greenland does not have any of the volcanic hot springs at ground level that Iceland does. And not only fissures serve as their beginning point. The summer sun opens vertical shafts called "moulins"—and these can plunge hundreds of feet down into the melting ice. Inside, they glow with bluish light. After a summer snowfall, a crust of snow can cover the tops of these moulins, creating a more perilous place for explorers to fall even than a fissure, since the latter are at least sometimes narrower. Both the fissures and the moulins expand and sometimes join together as the summer melting continues. This can create quite large caves.

These glacier caves, dry in the morning, may fill completely with meltwater by the afternoon. So cavers know to explore them in the morning only. The caves are constantly being remodeled by the flowing water, too, with walls occasionally collapsing.

Greenland cavers offer advice: Do not breathe in too many ice crystals, since they can actually cause suffocation. (The crystals splash up like a thin haze from waterfalls under the glacier in these sometimes tightly enclosed places.) Never shout—even sound waves can destabilize the walls enough to make one collapse. Take care in order to contemplate the unique beauty of these caves hewed of ice. By winter, Greenland's ice caves all vanish into solid ice, unlike Kverkfjöll in Iceland.

About a week after the visible steam and ash appeared, the "body" of the glacier itself swelled. It is hard to imagine the force required to lift up a section of a glacier that is nearly as large as Lake Ontario, but volcanism is that force. The dramatic new event that proceeded from this swell will be described in the next section.

Though people who live anywhere near the Vatnajökull on the country's south-coast area had long since evacuated safely (no Icelander has been killed by a volcano for more than 200 years), geologists were beginning to take more direct measurements. Later, they were able to report that, over the eruption's 13 some days, approximately .7 cubic mile (3 km³) of glacial ice had been melted by the volcanic heat. An extensive ridge of volcanic material, 3.5–4.25 miles (6–7 km) long, also formed under the Vatnajökull. They were also able to estimate that the volcanic material that broke through the glacier and became airborne was only 1 to 2 percent of the total mass of magma emitted in the eruption. And they measured the crevasses or cracks on the surface of the Vatnajökull: Some were 2.5 to five miles (4 to 8 km) long.

Most of the effects of the eruption, though, were invisible, hidden under the ice. Many glacier caves, as well as cauldrons and canyons, were surely created there by all the rushing meltwater. Geologists estimate that this hot water flowed under the ice for a full five weeks. But these caves—none of which was ever observed, even remotely—would have solidified back to ice again as the under-ice area cooled. There are no hot springs in this section of the glacier, as there are near Kverkfjöll. The refreezing of the ice after a volcanic eruption is called "the healing" of the glacier. Here, that took about a year.

WHEN A GLACIER SWELLS

Imagine the force of the water mass created as the glacial ice melted in this double volcano eruption of 1996 under the Vatnajökull glacier: It was enough to raise the glacier itself 50–65 feet (15–20 m) higher over the Grimsvötn volcano. Thirty-five days after the eruption began (and about 20 days after it ended), this water broke through an ice "dam" to race toward the sea. In Iceland, these are called *jökulhlaups*, or outburst floods; the word means "glacier run."

Of course glaciers "drool" water regularly, especially in summer. And every four or five years or so, the Vatnajökull flushes out extra fluid—about a billion tons of water—over several days. This is considered an "ordinary" jökulhlaup. They originate in some of the regular, smaller eruptions of the same active two Bardardunga and Grimsvötn volcanoes under the ice and of the other five volcanoes that accompany them underneath.

But the late 1996 flood was not at all ordinary. It was the most forceful in 60 years. From underneath the Vatnajökull glacier, out rushed .8 cubic mile (3.4 km³) of water. It flowed at a rate equal to three to five

Niagara Falls, all at once. At its peak, about 529,720 cubic feet (15,000 m³) of water raced out—every second. This was an epic jökulhlaup.

Icelanders are far from stupid. People do not live on the plains between the Vatnajökull glacier and the sea, and no one has been killed here by a jökulhlaup since 1898 (though there have been many of them). The floodplain is a black lava desert on which only the occasional plant is able to grow between onslaughts. But the country's main highway, which circles the country, and its many bridges and telephone poles do need to be there. (They cannot go over the glacier or through the sea.) In the jökulhlaup of 1996, every bit of this infrastructure was swept away.

Both scientists and tourists, up in airplanes, came to watch. One group of Icelandic geochemists analyzed the chemistry of the meltwater and found some 50 minerals in it that had originated deep within the Earth and been emitted by the two erupting volcanoes. These included mercury, copper, and zinc as well as more common chemical constituents such as carbon dioxide and, of course, water. It has long been known that much of the carbon dioxide and water that has ever formed on the planet, from the days of the early Earth, also came up through the mouths of volcanoes. Without them, there would not be life as humans know it on this planet. (And with more of them, we would add to our water supply, though also our carbon dioxide supply, a *greenhouse gas*.)

WHAT ELSE ICELANDIC GLACIERS DO

Beyond the glacier cave building, hidden eruptions, and very visible floods, glaciers here are actually helpful to people. The regular, daily glacier river flows created by the Vatnajökull are used to supply a great deal of the country's electric power. And a large glacial lagoon, punctuated by ornate icebergs bobbing out toward the nearby sea, is a major tourist attraction. Seals even swim in from the ocean to investigate.

THIS GLACIER IS HOT

Areas of the Vatnajökull glacier lie over hot springs, the ultimate source of the Kverkfjöll ice caves, as was described earlier. This is just one piece of evidence that establishes the volcanic nature of Iceland.

This country was created entirely by volcanoes. It rose up from the North Atlantic sea bed, lava piling upon lava upon lava, over 25 million years of undersea eruptions until the new land broke through the ocean's surface. The island continues to grow today. Iceland is not only piling up height over its interior from eruptions there, but it is also spreading out seaward from a broad zone that runs through the country north to south-central, then swings to the west. This is called the Neo-Volcanic Zone, the most volcanically active part of the country.

The source of this volcanism is twofold: a *hot spot*, a persistently active tectonic area originally deep within the Earth, and a *plate* boundary. The hot spot that made the country and continues to expand it now lies right under the northwest corner of the Vatnajökull glacier. The plate boundary—where the North Atlantic plate and the European plate are spreading apart—also is found in the Neo-Volcanic Zone, part of which is also under the Vatnajökull. These plates are what create the Neo-Volcanic Zone, naturally.

Iceland's Neo-Volcanic Zone, or spreading center, is moving to the east gradually—and it also "jumps" once every 6 to 8 million years. Actually, the zone only appears to move. It is the landmass, Iceland itself, which is moving over the hot spot. And the North Atlantic plate is also moving relative to the European plate. (See chapter 5, Kazumura Cave of Hawaii, the United States, for more on how this process works.)

WHAT CAUSES THE "HOT SPOT"

Geologists believe that Earth has about 37–49 volcanic hot spots. The ones under Iceland and Hawaii are the two most vigorous ones on Earth today. The "lifetime" of a hot spot seems to be about 130–150 million

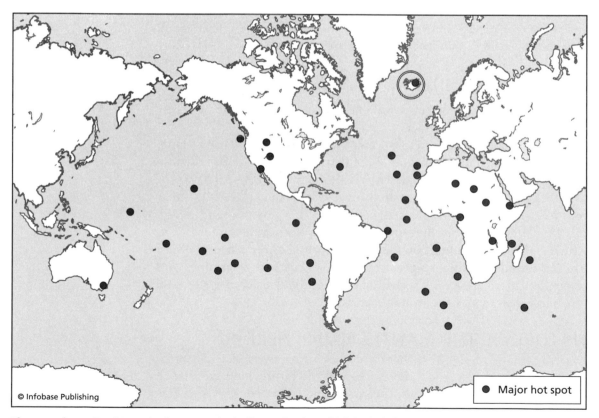

The map shows Earth's major hot spots, including Iceland's, which is circled.

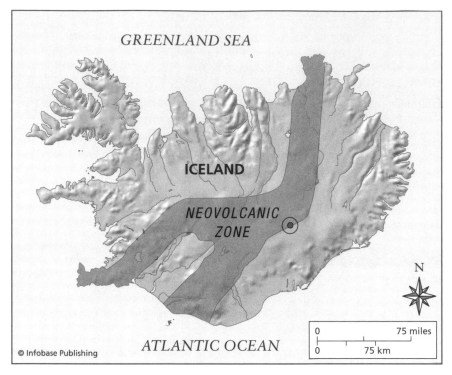

This schematic shows a basic model of the layers of our planet.

years. Iceland's have been active for about 100 million years, so far. Their handiwork is likely to continue.

The hot spot that helped to belch out Iceland is here because a plume of molten material in the mantle of the Earth lies under Iceland. Mantle plumes in general are so deep down—62–1,800 miles (100–2,900 km)—that they are invisible. But they are known to have thick "heads" at their tops (closest to the Earth's surface) and thinner tails (lower down). These mantle plumes are upwelling areas created by turbulent motions deep within the viscous, boiling hot, rocky, gassy mantle of the planet. (Water, too, has turbulent motions such as boiling, river currents, whirlpools, and waves, but these are more short-lived because the density of water is so much less than that of the mantle material.)

NATURE OF THE MANTLE PLUME HERE

How the mantle plume works here is a major area of research and controversy among geologists today. Researchers of the future will have a lot to say about it too. Its importance is considerable: What comes up via this hot spot in Iceland, and how it does so, is one of the best snapshots humans will ever have of what lies deep within the Earth. No one will ever be able to go down to see—a body would burn to cinders and be crushed flat before getting deep enough to be anywhere near the Earth's mantle.

Safe on the Earth's surface, geologists study the mantle plume here in various ways. First, they examine old earthquake records. Iceland has long been "wired" with *seismometers*—about 30 of them scattered across this small country—to monitor the deep earthquake volleys that precede, and thus warn us about, volcanic eruptions. These faint earthquakes are usually not detectable on the surface without these instruments. Geologists also create their own seismic waves to probe deliberately—by exploding dynamite in deep holes, then watching the vibrations recorded on the seismographs. Seismic evidence is useful because the signal changes its speed and its shape depending upon the nature of the rock it goes through. It is like a giant, silent ultrasound used in a hospital. It is also important because it allows people to know when an eruption is imminent—and to get out of the way.

Since the mantle plume area of research is so active now, new findings are probably coming in as you read this chapter. The picture is still intriguingly muddled, especially details about how the Earth's mantle is layered. Is there a discontinuity (a change in the viscosity or thickness of the molten material) at about 650 miles (1,050 km) down, under the hot spot here? Does this exist elsewhere? How do this, and other such transition zones, work? Is the layering different under Iceland than in other places? Does the main turbulence flow up from the mid-mantle, the lower mantle, or the upper mantle? Can mantle plumes be bent or deflected, probably at more than 620 miles (1,000 km) down, by "mantle winds" as they rise? Does one plume "feed" more than one hot spot? Are there "superplumes"? Are the changes in the layering of the planet's mantle all caused by differences of heat, or are there major chemical differences that may affect them? Why do mantle plumes make their large-scale movements, and how might we understand these patterns? Exactly how does mantle plume activity fit in with plate tectonics? Geologists work on questions like this, here in Iceland and elsewhere.

Yet another question about these plumes leads into the issue of the future of Earth as we know it: Do the broader processes of plate tectonics drain heat from the mantle, while mantle plumes drain heat from the *core* of the Earth, even deeper? If they do, these plumes will, eventually, cool the interior of the Earth completely. At that time, millions of years into the future, all tectonics would grind to a halt: There would not be anymore volcanoes, hot springs, earthquakes, or even new mountains. Erosion would then gradually break down the planet's higher elevations, until everything became a single flat plain, all over the Earth. Only glaciers would break the monotony.

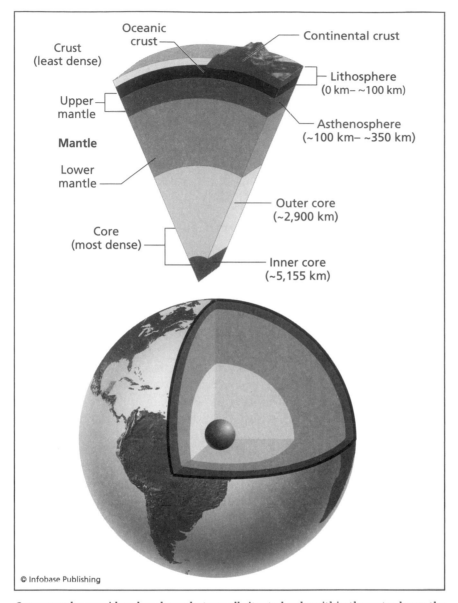

Caves may be considered as dense but are all situated only within the outer layer, the crust, of the planet.

EXTREMOPHILES IN KVERKFJÖLL?

As has been mentioned in earlier sections of the book describing extremophiles, these ancient creatures have been found in hot springs aboveground in Iceland and in suspended animation in the ice of Antarctica. They are probably also in the hot springs under the Vatnajökull glacier, the ones that melt the ice to form the Kverkfjöll glacier cave. These volcanically created springs are themselves ancient, probably about 25 million years old in this location, as old as the oldest lava flows here and much older than the glacier itself. Hence, these tiny creatures could well have been living here since then. Other species of extremophiles might be frozen into the Vatnajökull ice as fossils. Though the glacier is only about 2,500 years old, ice cover has probably existed at the highest elevations in this area for a couple of million years, and the creatures might be even in the oldest areas.

Geologists conjecture that fossil extremophiles could exist on the Moon also. They might be found in the permanently dark areas near the Moon's north and south poles, where the rims of ancient, probably volcanic, craters lie in shadows. This darkness would have protected the extremophiles from the ultraviolet sunlight, which probably would have either "fried" or evaporated them. Gas fumes from ancient volcanoes on the Moon could easily have created amino acids out of the methane, ammonia, sulfur, tungsten, carbon dioxide, and water they emitted. Amino acids could also have been brought in by meteorites. Similar situations might exist on Mars and on Jupiter's moon Io, as well as elsewhere in the solar system. These amino acids are the building blocks of life and could have led to extremophiles on other bodies the way they almost certainly have on Earth. Extremophiles, as has been described in various sections of the book, are an intriguing, relatively new area of research, with plenty of opportunities for the geologists of the future.

IN THE FIELD: ANALYZING VOLCANIC TREMORS

As was mentioned in earlier sections, earthquake volleys, also called volcanic tremors, usually occur before a volcanic eruption here. The proximate source of these tremors deep within the Earth is an area of research for geologists, including those who studied the 1996 eruption under the Vatnajökull glacier. They are trying to figure out whether these sudden, small movements are caused by molten fluids swishing in the tubelike paths that "feed" an eruption, or by fluid movements in the cracks of below-surface rocks, or by boiling groundwater, or by blobs of magma of different shapes doing a kind of quiver. These movements are very complex mathematically, occurring in what sometimes look like chaotic bursts and sometimes like regular volleys from an immense pop gun.

The tremors under the Earth at the Vatnajökull lasted for two days before the 1996 eruption. They were mostly small, except for one earthquake of 5.6 magnitude (still not an exceptionally large earthquake). During and after the eruption, more tremors occurred but decayed, or faded, differently.

Geologists used the data printed out automatically by the 30 different seismographs permanently positioned on the landscape to try to figure out exactly what was going on down there under the glacier and under the volcano under the glacier. They then used every mathematic tool available, including elaborate graphing and equations designed to describe chaotic natural processes. Their best estimate is that magma flowed smoothly up through a narrow cylinder-like space, then developed turbulent clumps that pressed explosively on the surrounding rock, then smoothed again. The smooth flow is called a laminar flow in physics, and the turbulence caused by flow into a narrow tube is called the Bernoulli effect.

Nothing that readers have learned in mathematics and physics classes, or will learn in later mathematics and physics classes, would ever be wasted in the study of geology. Neither would chemistry, nor ancient history, nor even an appreciation of natural beauty. And neither would a love for climbing around on rocks, in caves and elsewhere. Geologists love to learn about the Earth itself.

The Kverkfjöll ice cave is an excellent example of the kind of amazing surprises geology brings. It is a cave carved out of the ice of a glacier by the heat of a volcano.

Conclusion

Caves

This book has presented 10 caves in an exploration of the geology of this landform. Limestone caves are the most common on Earth, and so seven chapters have explored them: chapter 1, Mammoth Cave of Kentucky, the United States; chapter 2, Cenotes, Chicxulub, and the Caves of Yucatán, Mexico; chapter 3, Lascaux Cave of France; chapter 4, Lubang Nasib Bagus and the Sarawak Chamber of Malaysia; chapter 7, Carlsbad Caverns of New Mexico, the United States; chapter 8, Waitomo Cave of New Zealand; and chapter 9, Wind Cave of South Dakota, the United States. Of these, all but one, Carlsbad Cavern, formed almost entirely by the action of rainwater dripping through soil to form carbonic acid, which then gradually dissolved the limestone rock. Carlsbad's formation is the result of an additional acid, sulfuric acid, present in the cave because of oil and gas deposits buried in the rock; however, carbonic acid also contributed much to its formation. Two of the caves in the book formed as a result of the movements of magma, flowing lava. These are described in chapter 5, Kazumura Cave of Hawaii, the United States, and chapter 6, Fingal's Cave of Scotland, Great Britain. And one cave formed within a glacier: detailed in chapter 10, Kverkfjöll Cave of the Vatnajökull Glacier, Iceland.

Every cave, though, is in some way the footprint of water. Over huge spans of time, rainwater percolates through soil, followed by streams and rivers as additional architects in some cases and always to a lesser extent than the dripping water. The flowing lava that made the volcanic caves would not flow without water vapor, the primary gas in lava. Neither would the ice of a glacier form, then melt in places to open a cave of that kind.

And every cave is a peephole into the planet, the handiwork of time. Time deepens the cave as the *water table* drops lower, opening the now-dry upper passageways. Some caves, such as Mammoth Cave, are millions of years old, while others, such as Kazumura Cave, are only a few hundred years of age. Time is the other architect, forming first the caves and then hosting the *speleothems* within them; these unique cave formations, of incredible variety, depend upon the temperature and humidity of the cave as well as with the array of cracks and composition of the rock.

No cave lasts forever. Every one will suffer collapse eventually, though millions of years may be required.

Caves can be extreme environments too. And in them are often found species of creatures as old as any known on Earth, the *extremophiles*. These are keys to the early Earth and probably even to the nature of other planets and moons in our solar system.

Most of the caves on our own planet have not yet even been discovered, much less explored and fully mapped. Since most caves are limestone, part of a *karst terrain*, it is worth looking in that kind of place, an area of *sinkholes* and disappearing streams. Many limestone caves, however, their openings concealed and their territory untraveled, may never be discovered. Neither probably, will all the lava caves and glacier caves on Earth.

It is certain, though, that those who lack an understanding of cave geology will never discover a cave, or explore a known cave to find more passageways and chambers, or even fully enjoy an ordinary but extraordinary cave tour. Fortunately, readers of this book do indeed now have that basic understanding.

Nothing that readers of this book have learned will be wasted in the study of caves or of any landform of our planet. We live on an unquiet planet with pyrotechnic volcanoes, rumbling earthquakes, mountains eroding to the sea, rivers rushing, water dripping, ocean trenches ripping open, canyons cracking into rock, silent stones hiding their stories, and much more. It is worthwhile to learn geology in order to understand it more fully.

Glossary

a'a lava   rough, jagged type of lava

bedding planes   flat surfaces that separate strata, or layers, of rock in rock formations and reveal the sequence in which they were deposited

biofilm   living layer made by colony of bacteria or other microbe

calcite   a crystalline form of calcium carbonate; most SPELEOTHEMS are made of it

caldera   large depression in the ground caused by the collapse of a volcanic magma chamber

Cambrian   period of geological history from about 500 to 460 million years ago when the oceans covered much more of the world than they do today

Carboniferous   period of geological history from about 350 to 270 million years ago when the early Appalachians, early Alps, and early Himalayas began to form

cave   a natural opening beneath the Earth's surface

Cenozoic   epoch of geological history from about 70 million years ago through today when TECTONIC ACTIVITY and seafloor spreading were vigorous; includes the PALEOCENE, EOCENE, OLIGOCENE, MIOCENE, PLIOCENE, and PLEISTOCENE eras

core   deepest and densest part of the Earth; includes the liquid outer core and the 1,800-mile-(2,900-km-) down solid inner core, both primarily made of pure metal

Cretaceous   period of geological history from about 135 to 70 million years ago when dinosaurs ruled, both South America/Africa and Australia/Antarctica separated, and the Rocky Mountains began to form

crust   outermost layer of the Earth that varies from 12.5 miles (20 km) to 45 miles (70 km) thick, depending upon location on the planet *cueva* cave, Spanish

Devonian   period of geological history from about 400 to 350 million years ago when sea creatures ruled and the first land animals evolved along with the land vegetation

dripstone   cave formation made by dripping water

Eocene   period of geological history from about 60 to 40 million years ago, during which the climate of the world ended its warm period

escarpment   a ridge of land (low up to quite high) created by plate tectonic uplift

extremophile   ancient microbe found in extreme environments

faults, faulting   cracks or fractures in rock that show that the two adjacent sections have moved relative to each other

flowstone   cave formation made by flowing water

fossil passages   passages in caves that are no longer being extended by natural processes of cave formation

geochemistry   branch of geology that uses primarily chemistry in its research

geophysics   branch of geology that uses primarily physics in its research

GIS (geographic information systems)   hardware/software systems that bounce signals off satellites; they allow us to determine our exact location

greenhouse effect   climate pattern in which gases such as carbon dioxide lock in heat, warming the planet

gruta   cave, Spanish

halocline   water layer between heavier/saltier water and lighter/fresher water

helictite   cave formation (speleothem) that grows twisted, in ways that seem to defy gravity

Holocene   period of Earth history from about 10,000 years ago to the present when major new glaciation has halted; this period is often included as part of the PLEISTOCENE instead

hot spot   area where the Earth's CRUST is thinner, allowing plumes of hot MAGMA to force through, creating surface volcanoes and the land they make

isostatic rebound   the bouncing back of an area of Earth's CRUST after its depression by a heavy object such as a glacier

isotopes   related versions of chemical elements

joints   vertical cracks in rock masses

Jurassic   period of geological history from about 170 to 135 million years ago when volcanic activity was intense in the western United States, the Atlantic Ocean formed, and the continents moved close to their present positions on the Earth's surface

karst, karst terrain   surface features (e.g., sinkholes) indicating limestone-dissolution geology below

lava fountain   fiery gas and lava erupting out of a volcanic vent

lithosphere   solid top layer of the Earth's surface (including the CRUST and the outermost part of the MANTLE); about 62 miles (100 km) thick

magma   liquid, underground lava that can flow to the surface

magma chambers   underground reservoirs of molten lava

mantle   layer of the Earth between the CRUST and the CORE; composed of relatively dense rock

mantle plumes   large-scale turbulent motions in our planet's mantle

Miocene   period of geological history from about 25 to 12 million years ago when the Alps and Himalayas reached close to their present heights and the Appalachians and Rockies were in a period of erosion

Oligocene   period of geological history from about 40 to 25 million years ago when the Alps and Himalayas continued to grow and change and when FAULTING was common in the American West

Ordovician   period of geological history from about 500 to 460 million years ago when the ocean were more extensive than today and sea creatures were the predominant life-form; the same dates are used for the CAMBRIAN period

orogenic activity   the processes involved in mountain formation

pahoehoe   smooth, ropey type of lava

Paleocene   period of geological history from about 70 to 60 million years ago when the formation of the Rocky Mountains was largely completed and the landscape of the planet took on close to its present form

paleogeology   branch of geology that specializes in the most ancient parts of geological history

Paleozoic   epoch of geological history from about 500 to 225 million years ago; includes the CAMBRIAN, ORDOVICIAN, SILURIAN, DEVONIAN, CARBONIFEROUS, and PERMIAN

Pangaea   the supercontinent composed of the land of all present continents; it began to break up about 200 million years ago

Permian   period of geological history from about 270 to 225 million years ago when ice caps were extensive in the Southern Hemisphere

phytokarst   features created on limestone surfaces by plants (also called photokarst)

plate   large, rigid piece of the Earth's crust that moves across the surface because of turbulent plumes of MAGMA in the lower crust and mantle; plate interactions are the main force in the development of mountains, volcanoes, earthquakes, continental changes, even oceans; currently, geologists consider there to be seven major plates, eight medium ones, and about 20 smaller ones

plate tectonics   the study of the TECTONIC ACTIVITY of the Earth's PLATES

Pleistocene   period of geological history from about 2 million years ago to the present, when surges of glacial ice have been well documented

Pliocene   period of geological history from about 12 to 2 million years ago when PLATE interactions along the Pacific coast began

Precambrian   epoch of geological history from about 4 billion to 500 million years ago when the Earth formed as a planet, the crust developed, the first life-forms began in the sea, the early Appalachians formed, and the first ever glaciation occurred; Precambrian rocks have been documented in the SHIELD areas of most of the continents by PALEOGEOLOGY

precipitates   minerals removed from water through physical and chemical processes

rainshadow   the phenomenon in which the leeward side of a mountain or mountain range is starved of rain and snow since the windward side (usually the west side) receives virtually all the precipitation (as the mountains themselves block air masses, causing them to rise and cool, producing rain there)

Ring of Fire   zone at the edge of the Pacific Ocean worldwide where tectonic activity often occurs

sediments   the loose layers of soils, sands, muds, rocks, and decaying organisms that lie, for example, on the bottom of a body of water

seismic waves   underground waves such as those created by earthquakes that move through rock

seismographs   graphs showing tectonic activity underground, such as earthquakes

seismometers   devices used to create the seismographs

Silurian   period of geological history from about 460 to 400 million years ago when the earliest coral reefs formed in the sea

sinkhole   collapsed area at surface in karst terrain (cave may be below or near)

speleology   the scientific study of caves

speleothem   cave formation (e.g., stalactite, stalagmite)

stalactite   speleothem growing down from a cave's ceiling

stalagmite   speleothem growing up from a cave's floor

sump   cave passage filled with water

tectonic, tectonic activity, tectonic forces   related to the large-scale forces that move and shape extensive areas of the Earth's CRUST over long periods of time; examples include volcanoes, earthquakes, SUBDUCTION ZONES, FAULTING, mountain-building; caused by large plumes of seething magma below the crust

tephra   lava cooled to ash

Tertiary   geologic era from 70 million to 12 million years ago (includes the Paleocene, Eocene, Oligocene, Miocene, and Pliocene epochs)

tilt meters   devices placed on the surface in an area of tectonic activity that can detect a swelling of the ground

Triassic   the period of geological history from about 225 to 170 million years ago when TECTONIC ACTIVITY was common in the eastern United States

troglobite   creature that lives only in caves

troglophile   creature that lives in caves or elsewhere

trogloxene   creature that lives in caves but must leave the cave for food

tuff   solidified, weathered lava

vadose   cave passage made by a stream

vulcanism   volcanic activity

vulcanologists   scientists who study volcanoes

water table   the level below which water fills all the empty spaces

zone of saturation   underground zone permeated by water; below the water table

Books

Barr, Nevada. *Blind Descent*. New York: Avon Books, 1998. An excellent account of the Carlsbad Caverns area by a former National Park Service naturalist, in the form of a mystery.

Benyus, Janine. *Biomimicry*. New York: William Morrow, 1998. Describes the research being done that uses nature and natural systems as an inspiration and model for technological inventions.

Bullitt, Alexander Clark. *Rambles in the Mammoth Cave during the Year 1844, by a Visiter* (sic). Louisville, Ky.: Morton & Griswold, 1845. An account of what Mammoth Cave was like during various periods of its history.

Burnham, Brad. *Carlsbad Caverns*. New York: PowerKids Press, 2003. A similar treatment for Carlsbad.

———. *Cave of Lascaux*. New York: PowerKids Press, 2003. For younger readers, it provides the essentials, as well as more photographs of this cave.

———. *Kazumura Cave: The World's Largest Lava Tube*. New York: PowerKids Press, 2003. Yet another basic treatment, illustrated nicely, and on Kazumura Cave.

Carwardine, Mark. *Iceland, Nature's Meeting Place*. Reykjavík: Iceland Review, 1986. An excellent description of the natural history and landforms of the country in which Kverkfjöll ice cave is located.

Chernicoff, Stanley, and Donna Whitney. *Geology: An Introduction to Physical Geology*. Boston, New York: Houghton Mifflin, 2002. An excellent basic college textbook.

Courban, Paul, Claude Chabert, Peter Bosted, and Karen Lindsley. *Atlas of the Great Caves of the World*. St. Louis, Mo.: Cave Books, 1989. Filled with facts and lore on all types of caves around the world and the cavers who explore them.

de Watteville, Alastair. *The Island of Staffa*. Southampton, U.K.: Romsey Fine Art, 1993. Short and beautifully illustrated, this book provides the basics on the island where Fingal's Cave is located.

Erickson, Jon. *The Living Earth: Making of the Earth*. New York: Facts On File, 2001. A basic overview of geology for high school–age readers.

————. *The Living Earth: Rock Formations and Unusual Geologic Structures*. New York: Facts On File, 2001. A similar overview but with plenty of additional information.

George, Angelo I. *The New Madrid Earthquake at Mammoth Cave (1811–1812)*. Louisville, Ky.: George Publishing Company, 1992. A short account of a unusual event in the Mammoth area.

Gudmundsson, Ari Trausti, and Halldor Kjartansson. *Guide to the Geology of Iceland*. Rekyjavík: Bokautgafan Orn Og Orlygur, 1984. A guide to one of the most geologically interesting places on Earth—the country that is home to Kverkfjöll ice cave.

Hill, Carol A. *Geology of Carlsbad Caverns and Other Caves in the Guadalupe Mountains, New Mexico and Texas*. Socorro: New Mexico Bureau of Mines & Mineral Resources, 1987. Rather technical but includes plenty of good information on the geology of the whole area.

Hurd, Barbara. *Entering the Stone: On Caves and Feeling through the Dark*. Boston: Houghton Mifflin, 2003. Pleasingly literary, this book describes well the feelings one has as a beginning caver.

Levin, Harold L. *The Earth through Time*. Philadelphia: Saunders College Publishing, 1983. A good basic college text that provides an overview.

Logan, William Bryant. *Dirt*. New York: Riverhead Books, 1995. A good, short book on the science of dirt.

Mackenzie, Fred T., and Judith A. Mackenzie. *Our Changing Planet: An Introduction to Earth System Science and Global Environmental Change*. Upper Saddle River, N.J.: Prentice Hall, 1997. Another excellent college textbook, useful for context and detailed explanations.

Meredith, Mike, and Jerry Wooldridge. *Giant Caves of Borneo*. Kuala Lumpur, Malaysia: Tropical Press Sdn Bhd, 1992. Astounding pictures and excellent information about the area in which the Sarawak Chamber is found.

Moore, George W., and Nicholas Sullivan. *Speleology, Caves and the Cave Environment*. St. Louis, Mo.: Cave Books, 1997. Plenty of detail for those who want to get into caving.

Ong, Johnny. *Mysterious Caves of Langkuwi, Malaysia*. Selangor, Malaysia: Department of Irrigation and Drainage, Ministry of Agriculture, 1994. Excellent descriptions of all the major caves in an area of Malaysia not too far from the Sarawak area.

Parker, Ronald B. *Inscrutable Earth*. New York: Charles Scribner's Sons, 1984. An essay-like book that encourages readers to love geology.

Patent, Dorothy Hinshaw. *Mystery of the Lascaux Cave*. New York: Benchmark Books, 1999. Provides the basics of the mystery of the Stone Age art in Lascaux.

Radlauer, Ruth. *Carlsbad Caverns National Park*. Chicago: Children's Press, 1981. For younger readers, the book describes the cave and includes nice illustrations.

Roberts, David, and Jon Krakauer. *Iceland, Land of the Sagas*. New York: Villard Books, 1990. An adventurous and stunningly beautiful treatment of Iceland, where Kverkfjöll ice cave is situated.

Schneider, Bill. *Hiking Carlsbad Caverns and Guadalupe Mountains National Parks*. Helena, Mont.: Falcon, 1996. Presents all the interesting belowground and aboveground exploration ideas.

Tarbuck, Edward J., and Frederick K. Lutgens. *Earth, An Introduction to Physical Geology*. Upper Saddle River, N.J.: Prentice Hall, 1999. Another basic textbook for perspective and detailed explanations.

Taylor, Michael Ray. *Caves, Exploring Hidden Realms*. Washington, D.C.: National Geographic Books, 2001. Inspirationally elegant photographs and text.

Time Almanac 2004. Needham, Mass.: Pearson Education, 2003, passim. Plenty of diverse facts to plumb.

Vernon, Ron. *Beneath Our Feet: The Rocks of Planet Earth*. Cambridge: Cambridge University Press, 2000. Presents, in clear and pleasant photographs, ways to identify rocks.

Wallace, David Rains. *Mammoth Cave*. Washington, D.C.: U.S. Department of the Interior, 2003. Official facts and statements about the longest cave in the world.

Wolfe, David W. *Tales from the Underground: A Natural History of Subterranean Life*. Cambridge, Mass.: Perseus Publishing, 2001. Essay-like, this book will delight readers with a variety of Wolfe's experiences.

World Atlas, Millennium Edition. New York: DK Publishing, 1999, passim. Another wonderful source of maps and facts, to place cave areas in the context of their countries.

Wyckoff, Jerome. *Reading the Earth: Landforms in the Making*. Mahwah, N.J.: Adastra West, 1999. Focusing on what can be seen aboveground, this book shows how to interpret what one sees on the planet.

Web Sites

American Cave Conservation Association

http://www.cavern.org/acca/accahome.html

Dedicated to the conservation of caves and related resources across the nation and around the world

Bat Conservation International

http://www.bat-con.org

Contains information on various species of bats, their environments, and conservation efforts, with an extensive list of further reading and resources

British Cave Research Association

http://www.bcra.org.uk

An organization in the United Kingdom that promotes, researches, and documents the nation's caves. The site contains links to the organization's reference library, as well as numerous articles on their publications on cave and karst science and studies.

Cave Books

http://www.cavebooks.com

A wide range of cave-related books

The Cave of Chauvet-Pont-d'Arc

http://www.culture.fr/culture/arcnat/chauvet/en

From the French Ministry of Culture and Communication, this site details the discovery and documentation of ancient cave art in a recently discovered cave in France.

Cave Research Foundation

http://www.cave-research.org

Dedicated to documenting, studying, and protecting caves and karst resources

Caves.com

http://www.caves.com

A good site with information for those interested in caves, caving, and cave digging

Earthwatch

http://www.earthwatch.org

Organization that allows anyone to accompany a scientist while conducting research, with several cave study tours.

Hawaii Institute of Geophysics and Planetology

http://hotspot.higp.hawaii.edu/goes

This site has an image database of geological hot spots and volcano sites, updated via satellite image every 15 minutes.

Icelandic Speleological Society

http://www.speleo.is/about_iss.htm

General information about caves and caving in Iceland

Inside Earth

http://www2.nature.nps.gov/geology/caves/newsletter.htm

This site has news from all national parks that have caves, whether or not that is the main attraction

Lascaux Cave

http://www.culture.fr/culture/arcnat/lascaux/en

Also provided by the French Ministry of Culture and Communication, this site contains detailed information on the prehistoric people of Lascaux Cave and their artwork.

Mull and Iona Chamber of Commerce

http://www.zynet.co.uk/mull

Information about touring Staffa, the home of Fingal's Cave, and nearby islands

National Caves Association

http://www.cavern.com

Directories and information about caves and caverns open to the public in the United States

National Geographic Society

http://www.nationalgeographic.com

The online archives contain many articles and features about caves around the world.

National Speleological Society
http://www.caves.org
Dedicated to the study, conservation, exploration, and knowledge of caves

NASA's National Astrobiology Institute
http://nai.arc.nasa.gov
Dedicated to research about life in extreme environments on Earth and future plans for such environments in outer space

Show Caves of the World
http://www.showcaves.com
Site with data and maps on numerous caves that are open to the public throughout the world.

Speleobooks
http://www.speleobooks.com
Web site devoted to books specifically about bats and caves

Speleoprojects
http://www.speleoprojects.com
Resource catalog providing many books, magazines, videos, and other publications relating to caves

United States Geological Survey: Geologic Time
http://pubs.usgs.gov/gip/geotime
An index of articles with information on the geologic timescale and natural history

The Virtual Cave
http://www.goodearthgraphics.com/virtcave.html
A virtual tour tells the story of caves through pictures and information about four different cave types.

The Virtual Museum of Bacteria-Extremophiles
http://www.bacteriamuseum.org/niches/evolution/extremophiles.shtml
This site contains both general and in-depth information on bacteria and extremophiles for the general public as well as researchers.

Magazines
and Journals

Note to readers: This bibliography of magazines and journals has been prepared in a different fashion than is typical because it is designed to be especially educational for readers. Though every specific journal reference is available from the author, upon request, these are not detailed here—high school readers working online to research the geology of lakes in this volume may find newer references by the time the book appears. Instead, the author is hereby guiding readers to the best sources in general, including the top journals found most useful in writing this book and the best science periodicals, where the newest material is explained in context, weekly or monthly. These sources are prioritized, categorized, and described so that readers may learn from them. As a former high school teacher, the author believes that this kind of working bibliography will serve readers best.

Magazines for the general public, consulted regularly in the writing of this book, and worth looking at regularly, for those interested in geology or any other science:

Earthwatch Institute Journal
3 Clock Tower Place, Suite 100
Box 75
Maynard, MA 01754
http://www.earthwatch.org
Takes readers to research sites around the world and describes them in detail

National Geographic
1145 17th Street, NW
Washington, DC 20036-4688
http://nationalgeographic.com/ngm
Highly illustrated magazine that also includes plenty of interesting information on expeditions, caving, and other items

National Parks
1300 19th Street, NW
Suite 300
Washington, DC 20036
http://www.npca.org/magazine
Covers research and other news from America's national parks

Natural History
36 West 25th Street, Fifth Floor
New York, NY 10010
http://www.naturalhistorymag.com
An excellent general interest magazine on this subject, which includes plenty of information about landforms

Nature
345 Park Avenue South, 10th Floor
New York, NY 0010-1707
http://www.nature.com
One of the top journals in the world, with geology articles appearing regularly

New Scientist
6277 Sea Harbor Drive
Orlando, FL, 32887
http://www.newscientist.com
A general interest weekly science magazine with descriptions of up-to-the-minute research findings

Science
1200 New York Avenue, NW
Washington, DC 20005
http://www.sciencemag.org
The premier scientific journal in our country, it presents the latest research studies in all areas of science.

Science News
1719 N Street, NW
Washington, DC 20036
http://www.sciencenews.org
A weekly publication that covers the latest top research news, in all fields of science, in a truly superb fashion.

Scientific American
415 Madison Avenue
New York, NY 10017
http://www.sciam.com

A monthly publication that offers extended articles providing science perspective on subjects including geology, covers geology.

Sky & Telescope
49 Bay State Road
Cambridge, MA 02138-1200
http://www.skyandtelescope.com
Covers geology of other planets and, occasionally, extremophiles

USGS Information Services
Box 25286, Building 810, Denver Federal Center
Denver, CO 80225
Provides U.S. Geological Survey Reports and other material from the government agency leading the field

Magazines for the general public, consulted occasionally in the writing of this book and worth looking through occasionally for those interested in geology or any other science:

Descent (U.K.-based magazine)
P.O. Box 100
Abergavenny, NP7 9WY, United Kingdom
http://www.caving.uk.com/Resources/Pages/d_pages/descent.html
Covers cave sites and caving expeditions

Iceland Review
Borgart⁻ni 23
105 Reykjavík, Iceland
http://www.icelandreview.com
Offers amazing photographs of, and solid information about, this country's unusual landforms

Outside
400 Market Street
Santa Fe, NM 87501
http://www.outside.away.com
Describes adventures and expeditions in the natural world, in superb writing styles

Smithsonian
MRC 951, P.O. Box 37012
Washington, DC 20013-7012
http://www.smithsonianmag.si.edu/
Has extended articles about American subjects, occasionally geological in nature

Index

Note: *Italic* page numbers indicate illustrations.
C indicates color insert pages.